STRAWBERRIES IN THE GARDEN

Memories of my Early Years in Kingston upon Hull

DEREK T. PRITCHETT

Grateful thanks to my sponsors **DYSC IT Solutions** (info@dysc.co.uk)

Published by Derek T. Pritchett
Publishing partner: Paragon Publishing, Rothersthorpe
First published 2017
© Derek T. Pritchett 2017

ISBN 978-1-78222-526-3

Book design, layout and production management by Into Print
www.intoprint.net
+44 (0)1604 832149

Printed and bound in UK and USA by Lightning Source

DEDICATIONS

In pride of place, I must dedicate this book to my totally selfless Mother, whose (at times) unsuspecting influence shaped my early life, laying the foundations for all that I have accomplished. It was a real tragedy that her early death didn't allow her to appreciate the wonderful larger family that her outstanding example and influence helped so much to create.

The book is also dedicated to my wife, Sofia, without whose amazing support over these more than 40 years of marriage I wouldn't have been able to get to the point of writing this book at all. She has been an unwavering complement for all I have been able to do, and has played a very important role in building the magnificent family and home we have today.

My Father must also take a prominent place. On the one hand, it is only fair to accept that his sometimes obsessive personal dedication to voluntary interests made him seem a little aloof from the family on some occasions. Nevertheless, his example of honesty and transparency plus his every act at home (including all his carpentry work and gardening) made a great contribution to the family's progress and "wellbeing" in general.

My grandmother, Alice Smith, was the only grandparent of mine with whom I was able to maintain a close relationship for many years. She had been widowed just after the end of the War and lived on her own for the next 22 years. She had infinite patience with all her 5 grandchildren and would spend lots of time with me on my regular visits to her home in Stanhope Avenue.

[Here I must stress that I find it impossible to include any comments about my other 3 grandparents, for the simple reason that in two cases they died during my first four years of life, and in the case of Grandad Mills, he became bed-ridden and unable to speak properly when I was only 6 or 7].

I can appreciate however that Grandad Mills' life appears to have been dedicated to his wife and family, despite his long absences at sea and his very humble origins. I speculate in saying that most probably he found in them the warmth of the family that he never had as a child.

My twelve Aunts and Uncles each in their own way had a certain influence on my early life, which I will try to detail later in the thumbnail portrait of each couple that I have included. Surprisingly, only one of the eight marriages in our two families ended in separation or divorce, in a time when the amount of broken marriages soared to record heights.

Acknowledgements

First, I must thank our three offspring, who have made special journeys to contribute photos of the houses where several of their grandparents or great-grandparents lived in years gone by, and the one where I was born.

My sincere thanks also to various contributors to the Facebook pages *"Old Hull"*, (especially FL Sylvester) and *"Hull Areas, the Old Years"* from whom I have borrowed several photos to illustrate my parents' environment and early life in my birthplace.

An unusual "thank you" to Bianca Sofía Valero and Hannah Victoria Valero, our little granddaughters from Kalamazoo (Michigan), for coming into this world, and to their parents, Melissa (our daughter) and Luivi, who gave me the chance to be away from home in Colombia to "help out" after the birth. Without those four and a half months, when I was forcibly removed from the routine of the gardens and building work at Dapa and had the odd couple of hours spare from time to time, I would never have been able to make progress with this book to the point of sending it to print.

Foreword

I am writing this first part of my book, as also the second part which will follow later, in an attempt to leave for our grandchildren and future generations a kind of sketch of both my own life and what little I know or have learnt about earlier generations of the family, including what I have been able to compile of our family tree. It is first and foremost meant especially for the new generation of grandchildren of ours and of all my own cousins, who will know very little about our common grandparents and their ancestors, and precious little about me, I imagine.

Rather than being a literary exercise, it has been an effort to give a random account of our family predecessors and a few details of my own life during these past 70 years. Hopefully, I portray a vague vision of the world in which a few of our ancestors and I lived in the late 19th, the 20th and the 21st centuries.

"The reconstruction of knowledge about the past is the only way to generate a sense of belonging to a place [or a family]. To understand where we come from and what we are made of. A city [or in this case a family] cannot project its future with its back to the past." (A very apt quote from Omar Cubas, the leader of the successful historic centre restoration project at Asuncion, Paraguay).

The book is also meant to be a celebration of the fact that, over a relatively short period of time (maybe 4 generations) with a constant struggle for self-improvement, our families in general have been able to achieve greater comforts, better housing and a much better education, through their own personal efforts. On the other hand, we don't always recall and it is sometimes not always easy to understand, how our ancestors had to struggle so hard against the situations of war, of economic recessions and adverse living conditions to make progress in their search for a better life for themselves and their descendants.

On some rare occasions, progress has simply derived from being "in the right place at the right moment", but usually it has entailed much effort, study, great tenacity and sometimes even the need to face great dangers at sea to "get ahead" despite humble beginnings in the majority of cases. But I am proud to say that all these efforts have been very worthwhile.

To be honest, when I was young, I had no genuine awareness of the family's place in the world, its social status or its income level. We lived what I saw as a "normal life", attending a "normal" primary school, a "normal" local church and being encouraged to have "normal" ambitions for later life. Thus, I was fortunate not to feel the influence of the supposed constraints of a lower middle class life in the 1940's and 50's with all the restrictions of income and expenditure this usually entailed. In fact, I was to take charge of our family's weekly grocery shopping from the age of 8 and became very much aware (probably more than the average child of my age) of how the money was being spent on everyday goods. Even so, at the time, it seemed very "normal" the way that we seemed to live as a family.

The interesting part of the progress attained by our families over all this time has been the fact that the process has not been a ruthless pursuit of personal wealth, but a simple desire to achieve a better standard of living in general for all family members.

Although several family contemporaries (in my early life) would have been witnesses to many of the events I recall, almost all of them have now passed away, leaving hardly any record of themselves or life in their time. Additionally, even the part of my family that is still with us probably has little knowledge of the life I have experienced after being "banished to the jungle", as one person once bizarrely described my departure for Colombia. However, this period will be covered in the second part of the book.

I have tried to present my information as accurately as possible, but if any of my readers find any errors, I apologise most sincerely. I have attempted to research all facts about people, places and dates to the best of my ability, but with the passage of so much time since many of the events I relate, it is almost inevitable that there may be a few small mistakes in facts or appreciations.

SPECIAL NOTES:

It has been quite impossible to keep a strictly chronological order in all the different events I have related. This arises from an attempt to bring together people and places and their interrelationships, sometimes extending over a long period of time. Nevertheless, I trust that, in this way, my narrative will be more interesting to all as a result.

Additionally, I have included some paragraphs on subjects which may have no direct connection with my own life, but will help future generations to visualise the world of the different moments I have been writing about, especially the War years, which I consider so important in the appreciation of life in Britain in the second half of the 20th Century.

PERSONAL MISSION

One of my main aims in life has focused on a general desire to make a positive contribution to "developing things", both things of my own and things for others, though without any pretension to create really grandiose things – a fluency in languages; a good technique in table tennis; new products in the different marketing roles I held; new bilingual schools both for our own children and many others; a family with a special sense of independence and self-confidence; gardens full of fruit and flowers, and now a book full of family memories.

Having been very aware over time of the great efforts of our former generations to give the newer generations a better life, I have always tried to make special emphasis on furthering this goal. The search for happiness, fulfilment, and well-being for one's descendants has meant I have aimed to base my life on core Christian values, without necessarily being a member (as an adult) of any religious group. These core values, a legacy of my grandparents and especially my parents, have provided a framework for identifying, pursuing, and achieving those objectives that offer a long-term stability for the family and their descendants.

My greatest satisfaction has derived from observing the gradual fulfilment of many of these objectives, despite great sacrifices experienced at times by all of us in the family. No less has been the sensation derived from being worthy of the respect and admiration of family, friends, and business colleagues in the pursuit of these aims. Nevertheless, to what extent I have been able to accomplish these aims, I leave others to judge.

CONTENTS

Chapter 1

EARLIER GENERATIONS: MY GRANDPARENTS

The cities of Cardiff, London, Hull and the village of Preston (E. Yorkshire), are the four places that proved to be the sundry origins of people with their own local traditions, cultures and accents, whose lives eventually came together in an exceptional merger in the east of the city of Kingston upon Hull. These diverse roots would eventually form my personality, the legacy of my four grandparents, all born towards the end of the 19th century.

There are many important factors that help to shape a person's life, like genes, DNA, family background, ancestors' personalities, personal skills and attributes, relatives' experiences and adventures, or perhaps in many cases the interaction with school teachers, role models and other figures of authority. In my case, I can only conclude that my life seems to have been shaped by small contributions from many, if not all, of these complex influences.

Most certainly, I can identify the influence in my formation to a large degree from my Welsh mother, and then certain genes inherited from my father. Two of the role models were most certainly the minister from our local church when I was a young boy and a decisive non-family contribution from one particular teacher at my secondary school. He probably never appreciated the extent of his contribution to the diversity of my life, despite the fact that at one stage I managed to write to him to thank him for his extraordinary dedication.

However, let's first look back to the late 19th century, to the time when those four grandparents were making their first appearance in an extremely difficult world, which in the following 50 years would be convulsed by no less than the two World Wars. That way, I can try to fathom out which traits of character I might have inherited from each of my predecessors.

Gertrude Mabel JAMES (later MILLS)

On the Mills side of the family, we have Grandma Gertrude (Gertie) Mabel Mills (nee James). She was born in June 1891 in Cardiff, the eldest daughter of William Henry James and Jennet James. Her father William was a railway signalman. Gertrude's mother, Jennet James was born in 1866 in Neath, Wales, being the daughter of John H. James and Mary (surname not determined), and married William Henry James in 1889 in Cardiff.

Gertie with husband Fred (1920's?)

Gertie with daughter Doris (1916?)

William Henry, born in 1867, was the second child from the marriage of John James (not John H.) and Jane Bisgrove in 1863. His elder brother was Lewis A.B. James (from whom I assume my Uncle Trevor inherited one of his middle names – Lewis). Additionally, the family had four younger brothers and a younger sister, 7 children in all.

William's own father was James James, born in Nantygle, Monmouthshire in 1812, shown here in a photo from (probably) the 1880's, together with his son John and grandson William Henry, my own great grandfather. The adjacent photograph (date unknown) is of Lewis James proudly displaying a medal, accompanied by his wife Elizabeth.

The family home was recorded as South Luton Place, Cardiff in 1891 (see photos below of the houses as they are today).

Four generations

Lewis James & Elizabeth

William James' house at South Luton Pl., Cardiff

Fred & Gertie's house at 12 Malefant St, Cardiff

We know little about Gertie's upbringing, childhood or youth, except that she was the eldest of three sisters, all born in Cardiff, Annie M. James in 1893 and Hilda James in 1899. I would get to know Annie very well in my early childhood (see Chapter 10). However, although I did meet "little" Hilda on two occasions, I only have vague memories of a visit she made to us in Hull, probably in the mid-1950's.

Gertrude must have met my grandfather Fred Mills in the port of Cardiff on one of his spells of leave on land when he was in his late twenties. By some strange coincidence, Fred's mother's maiden name was also James. So, one could wonder if there were any distant relationship between the two families, though, being a relatively common surname, this is a very remote chance. They were married in Cardiff on 30th January 1912, and had the first of their four children, Doris Irene Mills, just 6 weeks later on 11th March 1912 in Barry, some 10 miles southwest of Cardiff. Thirty years later, Doris would become my mother in 1942.

Unfortunately, I have no true recollection of Grandma Gertie, as she died before I was 2 years old. I understand she was of medium height, a very kind, rather fragile lady, dedicated full time to her family.

Gertie & Frederick at my parents' wedding
(1937)

She suffered for many years with lung problems, from which she died at the early age of 52 in 1944, before the end of the Second World War. As with her two younger sisters, Annie and Hilda, she spoke with a soft but firm Welsh accent that she never lost during the 20-odd years she spent in Hull, away from her home town, Cardiff, the capital of Wales.

Grandma Gertie had four children, my mother Doris Irene the eldest, followed by Trevor Charles Lewis, who was also born in Cardiff, and Dinky (real name Gertrude Ethel) and Peggy, both born in Hull.

FREDERICK CHARLES MILLS

Grandad Frederick Charles Mills, a true Cockney, was born in central London (probably in the third quarter of 1881) in the District of Holborn, within the sound of Bow Bells. His parents were James Thomas Mills (from Middlesex) and Nancy May James, who was born in Gloucester, but died young at the age of 35, when her fourth son was only 6, and Frederick only 9.

Fred was the third of four brothers, in a family of fairly scant resources and with no mother when the eldest son was only 12. His father, James Thomas Mills, who was a prison warden at Newgate, seems to have been unable to cope with the four sons after his wife's death, and turned to drink. As a result, we understand that all four brothers (James Thomas, George Henry, Frederick and Albert) had no alternative but to leave home at an early age to be able to survive.

The four Mills brothers;
Frederick top right

The parents of my great grandfather James Thomas Mills, were Charles Mills, born in Staffordshire in 1813, and Margaret (whose surname we have been unable to define) born in London in 1815. Going back a little further to the mid-1700's, the two prior generations all came from Staffordshire.

It appears that Fred was sent away on (or left home for) a Training ship and must have taken a kind of apprenticeship to become a ship's cook and/or steward with the Blue Funnel Line around the age of 13 or 14, with Cardiff as the port he regularly sailed from. Ships of the Blue Funnel fleet all had names from classical Greek legend or history. The majority were cargo ships, but most of the Line's cargo ships also had capacity for a few passengers. The line also had a small number of purely passenger vessels.

One of Fred's elder brothers became a professional boxer, but nothing much more was ever known about him or the other two brothers. My Auntie Dinky is not completely certain, but she believes two of his elder brothers were in the army and may have eventually emigrated to settle in South Africa.

By the time I could really start to appreciate my grandfather, I was probably 6 or 7. He was a well-built man, of medium height, with a round reddish face, and obvious signs of his hard life at sea. He was not especially voluble, but by then, being just over 60, a very amiable grandfather. One of the ailments that his sea voyages had left him was malaria, which gave him regular bouts of sweating and trembling.

In 1948 or possibly 1949, he suffered a massive stroke, which, I assume, might have been one of the long-term consequences of his malaria and/or who knows what other ailments when at sea. The stroke was so vast that the whole of his left side was totally paralysed, his speech was almost impossible and it even made eating extremely difficult for him. This left him lying on a bed for several years before he died at around the age of 71 on March 23rd, 1953.

In hindsight, Fred's stroke and later his relatively early death were a great misfortune for me, his grandson, in the sense that they deprived me of the opportunity to have listened to a grandfather's tales about all his journeys to different parts of the world as a ship's cook or steward. It was even more poignant, when I started to learn Spanish, of which he almost certainly must have known at least a few words, as a result of his calls at South American and possibly Spanish ports. But, just before I was 11 (two years prior to me starting to learn Spanish), he had died.

My spirit of adventure seems to have been Fred Mills' legacy. His "apprenticeship", and afterwards, his work for just over 25 years as a Ship's Cook or Steward on the Blue Funnel Line would send him on 5-month long journeys out to the east (Africa and Asia) returning via the two coasts of South America, initially rounding Tierra del Fuego, before the opening of the Panama Canal. Whether his ships would have used the Suez Canal and thus called at Mediterranean ports, or would have taken the long route to the south of Africa, I'm not sure, but I hope these details will soon be put online, in the way that the passenger lists are now available for researching.

Fred certainly had a very full life on the coastal traffic steamers (cabotage, to use the French term) that called on all major (and probably many minor) ports on their route dropping off their cargo, and picking up more for other ports on the rest of their voyage. We can assume Fred may have had a special interest in Brazil, since on one of the voyages, he brought back from the Pernambuco region of Brazil a green and red parrot (named Joey), who lived for many years with my mother's parents in Hull and later, in the same house, with my Aunt Dinky and Uncle Albert. However much we all tried to get Joey to speak, he never uttered a single identifiable word! So, I guess we should have tried him out in Portuguese!

After those 25+ years at sea, part of which covered the First World War, Fred was ready for a somewhat less demanding land job, and decided to retire from seafaring in the second half of 1922. He must have been well thought of by the Blue Funnel Line, since, although they couldn't accommodate him in Cardiff (his port base and Gertrude's home town), they appointed him to the position of ship's purser in the port of Hull later that year or possibly in early 1923.

Thus, the family, then with their two children (Doris and Trevor) moved from their address at 41 Malefant Street, in Cardiff (see photo above) to the east coast port of Kingston upon Hull. There the Blue Funnel Line convinced the local City Council to assign them a new Council house on the housing estate that was being created along the recent extension to the east of Southcoates Lane called Preston Road. At this house (31 St. John's Grove), two new additions to the family would arrive: Dinky (real name Gertrude Ethel) born in late 1923, and Peggy, born in 1927.

That, then, was how a Cockney and his Welsh wife ended up living far away from their origins in a port in north-eastern England. I have learnt little about their lives as a couple either in their early marriage in Cardiff or with their family in Hull between 1923 and the year when my own parents got married at the neighbourhood church of St. Columba's on May 8th/1937. They obviously encouraged their offspring to attend the local church, as eventually they ended up being part of the parishioners who helped build the new church of St. Aidan, created originally as the place of worship for the new Preston Road estate.

HAROLD JOHN PRITCHETT

On the Pritchett side, we have Grandad Harold John Pritchett who was born in 1884, in what might now be called a "lower middle class" family in the city of Kingston-upon-Hull. How and why the family was based in Hull is a bit of a mystery, since over several generations and almost two centuries, there are roots that can be traced back to the area of Maidenhead, Kent.

Grandad Harold John became a watchmaker-repairer, though in 1901, at the age of 17, he figured in the census as an engineer's office clerk. He would seem to have made an adequate living with watches during all his married life. He played the banjo and the piano. Unfortunately, during WW2, his sight deteriorated to such an extent that he was almost blind. Many blame this on his intricate work with watches, but it is difficult to believe that this was the main cause. However, as a result of his loss of sight, he became extremely depressed and died in 1946 at the age of 62.

Our distant cousin Sir V.S. Pritchett in his famous autobiography "A Cab at the Door" admits to being baffled by the origins of the Pritchetts, having enjoyed the occasions when he stayed at his grandparents' "Manse" (church house) at Repton and in parts of north Yorkshire, but unable to fathom why they had settled there! He tells us in the book that his grandfather had been born in Hull, as his great grandfather had been a trawler seaman, all of whose brothers had drowned "between Hull and the Dogger Bank".

In the Pritchett heritage, I have sometimes seen in some of my relations part of what V.S. Pritchett described in so much detail and flair in his autobiography as a characteristic family trait:

"There is a strain of turbulence and insubordination running through our family: at any moment, all of us, though peaceable enough, are liable to stick our chins out and take our superiors down a peg or two if our pride is touched. We utter a sarcastic jibe especially at the wrong moment and are often tempted to cut off our noses to spite our faces, in a manner very satisfying to ourselves and very puzzling to amiable people. My grandfather was kindly enough, but one noticed that, at certain moments, he would raise one fine eyebrow dangerously, the eyes would widen into a fixed stare, the pupils would go small and look as hard as marbles, and the sharp arc of white would widen above them, as a horse's eye does when bolting. This is the moment of cold flat contradiction; also the moment of wit. And there is a grin at the startled face of the listener."

Harold John & Alice on their wedding day in 1911

Grandad Harold John & Grandma Alice in the early 1920's

ALICE MARY SMITH

Grandma Alice Smith married Harold John in Hull on 13th July 1911, a few months before my other grandparents were getting married in Cardiff. Alice and Harold John had a total of five children, though the second one (Doris) died at a very early age in 1918 (maybe during the terrific influenza epidemic?).

Legend has it that Alice Smith was born on a farm in the small village of Preston, East Yorkshire, a few miles to the east of Hull in 1886, although apparently her birth was registered at Sculcoates in Hull. Her parents were Harrison Smith (a blacksmith) and Agnes Mary Straker, whom he had married in 1885. Agnes was born in Preston (East Yorkshire), which gives a tangible link to this village. Not too long before her marriage, she was recorded as being a domestic servant at a farm in Burstwick, only about 3 miles from Preston. Unfortunately, again we know little about their immediate family and background, except that, before her marriage, Alice was an assistant in a "boot shop".

My grandmother, Alice Smith, was a tall lady (around 1.78 m) and with her long stride could walk several miles a day without seeming to get tired. She became a fascinating, placid influence, a kind of "confident" to many of my childhood exploits. Although when I was probably between 8 and 12 years old, I would first occasionally walk the mile and a bit from school to her house, once I got my bicycle at the age of 12, I would regularly ride round to 30 Stanhope Avenue to visit her. I might do the odd errand for her at the nearby shops on Holderness Road, or just sit down and chat about all and anything with her for an hour or sometimes much more. As she had lived on her own for so long, she seemed to enjoy my company and I loved to listen to her tales.

Her eldest child was Harold Alexander, born in October 1912, who, in 1937 at the age of 24, would marry Doris Irene Mills (Fred's eldest daughter) and later become my father. My paternal grandparents would go on to have three more children (Vera, Muriel and Dennis, in that order), about whom I will comment later on.

Although Alice's parents were living in Abbey Street (to the East of Hull) during the First World War, the Pritchetts (Alice and Harold John) and their family lived at Belgrave Drive (to the west of Hull) in the mid to late-1930's. After the Second World War, they had moved to a house in Stanhope Avenue, only several hundred yards away from the site where the new St. Aidan's church would be built.

Left to right (top): Grandad Harold John Pritchett, Grandma Alice Pritchett (Smith), Harold Alexander (bottom): Vera, Dennis & Muriel (around 1932)

View of Belgrave Drive, 2010

30 Stanhope Avenue (painted dark red), 2012

At some point in the late 1920's and early 30's, my other grandparents (the Mills) also encouraged their offspring to attend the same church, and participate in the youth activities of the time (the Scouts, the Guides, the Church Sunday School etc.). And it was during these activities to form the new chapel that, presumably, my own parents met up in the early 1930's. They were part of a common cause – organising activities to raise funds for the building of the new church of St. Aidan.

Although the previous paragraphs give a quick account of the origins of my immediate family, a recent ancestry search which I organised with the help of the Hull historian Ann Godden has given us a wider view of previous generations of the family. Restrictions of space have made it impossible to include these Family Trees in the book. However, I will have available for any family members who are interested separate sheets of updated Family Trees, showing ancestors starting in the 18th. century.

Chapter 2

EARLIER GENERATIONS: MY PARENTS

DORIS IRENE PRITCHETT (NEE MILLS)

My mother was born on March 11th, 1912 in the town of Barry, on the Bristol Channel, just 7 miles outside Cardiff, the capital of Wales, only two years before the outbreak of the first World War. Probably because of the War, she was baptised only in September of 1917 at St. Teilo's Church in Cardiff.

Her early childhood was spent principally with her mother, as her father Frederick Mills would be absent on his sea voyages for up to 5 months at a time. This would therefore explain the very strong and almost exclusive influence of Wales and Welsh traditions upon her. She was an only child for her first four and a half years until her brother Trevor was born. It was said she was a good pupil at her Primary School, and seems to have just started her secondary school in Cardiff around the time when her father decided to leave the sea and take an onshore job with the Blue Funnel Line far away in Hull.

The Shipping Line couldn't accommodate my grandfather in its Cardiff offices. Therefore, Doris and her younger brother Trevor would move to Hull with their parents, probably in the late summer of 1922, when she would be about 10½. I have no real recollection of her ever having talked about her secondary school in Hull, though obviously she would have attended one until at least the age of 14, as the law required at that time.

However, a recent search of old documents in my care turned up a letter of recommendation from the Hull Education Authority, certifying that Doris had attended "Southcoates Lane Girls' School" from 16th August 1922, and that:

"She is a well behaved, nicely mannered girl, industrious and intelligent, especially good in English; and of a willing and obliging disposition."

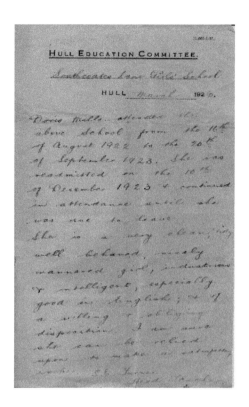

I must admit to never having heard of a school by that specific name, despite living in that area all my youth, and attending the very same school! However, contacts who are knowledgeable about this period now tell me that Southcoates Lane School, from its opening in 1912, was originally a mixed school, not only in the Primary and the Junior departments (as when I attended) but also in the Senior section, which, of course, would have only covered 3 years of tuition in the 1920's. Presumably, when the minimum school leaving age was increased to 16 at the end of the 1920's, the school wouldn't have enough space in the Senior section for both Girls and Boys. So, it became "Boys only". The girls were then transferred to Flinton High School, less than a mile away.

In 1924, Doris was also attending the Sunday School at St. Aidan's Church, which would still be in its temporary premises at that time. Then, when leaving school, in 1926, I speculate in thinking that she may have helped out at home with her younger sisters, Dinky, who would have been about 3, and Peggy, about to be born.

By the time Doris had reached her early 20's, she had a busy social life, including activities at the Church (St. Aidan's), the Sunday School and the Scouts. There she would be part of the young group who would be raising funds to build the new church and would be a great help for her "friend" Harold in his incipient work with the Scouts. At that time, my father had a "bicycle made for two" (could it have been the same one in the photo above which his parents had used?), then a motorbike with sidecar, and they would go out for rides on a weekend together. Dancing and outings to the cinema and theatre were also two more pastimes that would bring them together on many occasions.

Above: The house at 4 Telford Street, as it is today (image courtesy of Google). Below: 63 Telford Street, as it is today.

Exactly how long their courtship lasted I have no idea, but in 1936, Doris and Harold arranged to be married on May 8th, 1937. Although the new chapel of St. Aidan's was now built and in use, it had not yet been licensed to perform marriages. So, they had to be married at the nearby parish church of St. Columbas on Holderness Road at the corner of Laburnum Avenue. These details remain very prominent in my mind, as I would see them daily for some 20 years, displayed on a special plaque on the front of the huge radio set, which had been a wedding gift from the St. Aidan's Scout Group.

I believe they did have a honeymoon, but I never knew where. Then they set up their first home at 4 Telford Street, almost opposite the main entrance to East Park on Holderness Road. However, in the 1939 Census, they are registered as living at No. 63 of that same street (see Google images as these houses are nowadays).

Harold & Doris on their Wedding Day in 1937, with Bridesmaids Madge Blenkinsop (left) & Peggy Mills (right); Back Row: Jim Penny, Grandad Fred with Bridesmaids, Dinky Mills, Muriel & Vera Pritchett

My mother was a very outgoing woman, fond of children, but with a great strength of character. When she "knew what she wanted" for the family, she would do all in her power to fulfil her wishes, but was rarely impartial about things. She was proud of the social work that she devoted so much time to, both in the church and the Scouts. Throughout all her life, she never worked, in the usual sense of that phrase. However, as well as being a dedicated "homemaker", she was constantly devoting her time both in the day and evening to the organisation of different events which would raise funds for the Scouts and for the Church and Sunday School.

HAROLD ALEXANDER PRITCHETT

My father was born in Hull on October 2nd 1912. As I remarked earlier, the reasons for his family being in Hull or East Yorkshire are anything but clear. He was the eldest of a family of 5 children, though the second one (a girl named, ironically, Doris) died at a very early age. Thus, the Pritchetts always seemed to be a family of 4 children, since Doris's existence was never mentioned over all the years I would have regular contact with my grandmother and the Pritchett aunts and uncles.

As the family was living to the west of Hull at Belgrave Drive in Harold's early childhood, I assume he went to school in that area, though I must admit I never heard him talk at all about his school days. He must have moved with the family to the house I knew in Stanhope Avenue in the mid-1920's, since I have certificates from St. Andrew's Sunday School in East Hull, showing he attended there in 1924. Also we know he had links in his final adolescent years with the Scouts at St. Columba's Church, not more than 700 yards along Holderness Road from Stanhope Avenue.

What I did gather about his educational background relates to his night schools when he was a joiner's apprentice, studying very hard to aspire eventually to a professional level career. In fact, on more than one occasion, he won a free year's scholarship for his technical studies.

It would be a difficult 9 years between leaving school and leaving the family home to be married. Those were the pre- and post-recession years, when jobs were very hard to obtain and families faced all types of hardships, though little compared with the subsequent years of the Second World War.

The popularity of the Scout Movement in the 1920's must have attracted my father, since he joined the Troop at St. Columbas (though I'm not sure at what age), and was later a member of the Rovers (the over 16's) for several years. Then, with the creation of the new parish of St. Aidan's, he would devote time to forming this church's own Scout Group, which he would lead for over 30 years. The Second World War must have delayed my father's aspirations to be much more than just a carpenter, as I will explain in more detail in Chapter 4. However, he was finally able to make progress in his career in the early 1950's when he found himself a position as Builder's Manager with the company R. Finch & Sons of Hedon Road. However, on that I will also comment more fully in a later chapter.

In June of 1971, he was admitted as a Member of the Construction Surveyors' Institute, and was honoured to be named as President of the HULL GUILD of BUILDING for the year 1977/1978. Although he officially retired at 65 in 1977, Dad continued to work freelance doing surveying and costing projects for different building firms until very shortly before his death in 1988.

My father rarely talked about politics, as I guess he had little time to think about the problems of the world with so many responsibilities of his own! However, I do know that from the age of 21, he had voted Labour, probably out of the circumstance of being in a manual trade and surrounded by many trade unionists. After all, that was the time when the Labour Party was gaining popularity in most of Great Britain and especially in the North of England.

On the other hand, although I do know he was almost obliged to join a union in one of his jobs, he was not very keen on the way unions were run in the immediate post-war period. But, not long after he obtained his job as Builder's Manager, he switched his loyalties to the Conservatives, and on occasions in the 1960's openly voiced his approval of conservative policies.

Chapter 3

EARLIER GENERATIONS: MY AUNTS & UNCLES

As both my parents were the eldest of four children in each family, I had a total of six aunts and uncles. Here I include a brief thumbnail sketch of each couple.

VERA & JIM

On my father's side, his nearest sister was Vera, born in March 1918. From memory, I have the idea that after leaving school in the 1930's, she worked in one of the Hull City Council offices. However, once the War broke out, she enlisted in the armed forces to contribute to the "war effort". There she would meet, and later marry, Frederick James Tickelpenny, or Uncle Jim Penny, as we would all know him. Whether or not his surname was in fact Tickelpenny we never really were sure, though that was the anecdote I always heard, and recently it showed up in a BMD index as such.

Uncle Jim & Auntie Vera
on their wedding day (1941?)

Vera was an extremely highly strung person, probably as a result of her problems with hyperthyroidism. She was never able to have any children; so, when I was about 8 or 9, she and Jim decided to foster a young boy, called Ernest (Ernie) Moulden. At the time, he would be 4 or 5, and I would often go to Vera and Jim's prefab at 9 The Broadway, just off Holderness Road, to play with him.

Partly because of Ernie's own character and partly as a result of Vera's irritability, the relationship didn't prosper. On several occasions during the 8 or 9 years that Ernie was with Jim and Vera, he would be sent back to the orphanage and later would be given another chance. However, the original intention to adopt him never came to fruition.

Both Vera and Jim did social work as leaders of the Cubs at St. Aidan's Church. However, I always felt that Vera was a bit envious of my father's position in the same Scout Group as the overall leader. Therefore, over the years, we would be witnesses to a number of periods when there would be rows between them for seemingly petty reasons, or sometimes no apparent reason at all.

Prefabs, like the ones Vera & Muriel lived in

After I left England, and not long before the prefabs were going to be demolished, Vera and Jim bought themselves a house at 4 Mancklin Avenue on Sutton Road. However, Jim died suddenly of a heart attack not all that long after their move and although Vera lived on her own for several years, her thyroid problem eventually got the better of her.

MURIEL & NORMAN

My father's second sister was Muriel, born on March 9/1920. At the age of probably only 19 or 20, she joined the Armed Forces in the War, during which time she met Norman Carter, whom she married in October, 1945, with me as their pageboy, just over 3 years old.

Norman was born in the village of Zeals, Wiltshire and preserved his West Country accent throughout the whole of his life. As well as considering him as a very genial uncle at family encounters, I came to know him well as the very capable Manager of a grocery store (Field's) when I started to do shopping for the family at an early age at the Southcoates Lane shops. He went on to work at Carrick's before passing on to Lambert's in Whitefriargate (city centre) where he worked for many years, finishing his career at the Fine Fare Supermarket in Willerby Square (on the far west of the city), all stores in different parts of Hull.

Uncle Norman & Auntie Muriel on their Wedding Day in 1945, with me as Pageboy

Muriel & Norman lived for the first few months of their marriage as newlyweds at home with Grandma Alice, before moving, after the War, to the prefab on Preston Road (Hull) that they would occupy for most of their married life. They had two girls (Maureen and Elizabeth) in the fairly early part of their marriage. Finally, they moved to a small retirement bungalow on Holmpton Grove, only a few hundred yards away from the prefab.

Although they didn't have any boys, they were one of the couples who would devote a lot of time and effort to helping the Scout Parent's Committee in an impressive support for fund-raising events for Scouting activities at St. Aidan's. This would come to create a lifelong close relationship with my parents, who valued highly their selfless dedication.

DENNIS & HEATHER

My father's younger brother was Dennis John, born on September 12th, 1924. As a result of our close involvement with Scouting, I remember him first and foremost as a Scout Troop leader at St. Columba's Church. His working life was dedicated to the tugs on the Hull and Humber rivers, and he rose to become one of the principal Managers of the foremost tug company in Hull, The United Towing Co.

Uncle Dennis & Auntie Heather
on their wedding day

Dennis married Heather Rock on September 4th, 1948 at St. Aidan's Church, and they had two girls, Joyce (1949) and Anne (1951). However they finally got divorced in 1997, after almost 50 years of marriage. Dennis died in 2010 and Heather this year (2017) in February.

In a similar way to my father's relationship with Vera, Dennis would have differences with my father and our family which broke up their relationship completely after Vera's death and lasted till long after my father's death in 1988. Only a few years before Dennis himself died, I arranged to meet him again after almost 30 years of estrangement with our family. We talked over old times, but it was never possible to establish his real reasons for the rupture.

TREVOR & DOREEN

On my mother's side, her only brother was Trevor Charles Lewis, also born at Barry near Cardiff on 13th September 1916, when my Mother was just 4½. Before moving to Hull around the age of 6, he lived together with the rest of the family in Malefant Street, Cardiff in 1922. What always intrigued me was Trevor's third name "Lewis". However, now that I have historic details of the family tree, I speculate on this being a tribute to a great uncle Lewis Augustus Bisgrove JAMES, an elder brother of his grandfather on the Welsh side.

On leaving school in the early 1930's, Trevor was an unbound apprentice prior to the war at British Aerospace (then Hawker Siddeley aircraft factory) in Brough, to the west of Hull. Therefore, when he joined the armed forces at the age of 23, he went into the RAF.

Trevor was always very fond of the Spitfire planes, which had the more up-to-date Rolls Royce Merlin piston engine than the one the Hurricanes had. He had helped to build and assemble many of these at the Brough aerodrome including those flown to relieve Malta in WWII and then the ones for Ceylon (now Sri Lanka) before the Japanese tried to attack it. He was always into Hawker aircraft and built, assembled, fixed & maintained Hawker Hurricanes (piston) and Catalinas (Rotary) all through the war.

During his war service, he would use his self-educator books to start a new career. And while serving in places like Ceylon and the Maldives, he managed to find time to be able to study, teaching himself how to sail dinghies and small yachts whilst there. He completed his career studies during the war by correspondence whenever he was able, so that he could begin his full time Environmental training when he returned with direct practical experience. He did this rather than taking an option he had of going to work for Qantas in Australia.

His original position in Hull as Public Health Inspector became an Environmental Health Inspector with all 5 "Tickets", which was quite unusual as most Environmental degrees would be in a single ticket space only. With these qualifications, he was later promoted to District Environmental Officer for the area covering Bridlington, Filey and Scarborough.

Trevor was a great dancer. So, I believe he met his wife, Doreen Hadfield, when having nights out at one of several popular dancehall venues that East Hull sported in the post-war era. Doreen was born in Hull on 28th January 1928 and her family lived in Balfour Street, not far from where some of my Pritchett relations lived till being bombed out during the war.

Trevor & Doreen's Wedding in 1952

Not long after being married on August 2nd, 1952, Trevor and Doreen went to live in a very comfortable house in Kingsley Avenue, where they had their three children, Robert (Bob), Lesley and Shirley. Then in 1963, they moved to a new private estate called Sandsacre in Bridlington, when Trevor was promoted to his regional supervisory position.

Trevor was a very serious contemplative person, with whom I always got on very well. On many of the occasions when we saw each other, he would often comment on his experiences in the War and in his early career. Unfortunately, with his move to Bridlington and then my move to Colombia, I didn't have as many opportunities to see him as I might have wished.

I managed to keep regular contact with the Mills', even after Uncle Trevor's death, travelling to Bridlington whenever I was on holiday in Britain, sometimes on my own and often with Sofia. Doreen would always put on a lovely meal to greet us and we would listen to her conversation for most of the afternoon.

DINKY & ALBERT

My mother's elder sister, Dinky, whose real name is Gertrude Ethel was born on November 29th at 31 St. John's Grove not long after the family moved to Hull in 1923. At the moment of writing, she still lives in the same house after almost 94 years, having had it passed on to her and her husband Albert, when our Grandad Fred died in 1953. From what I can judge, she must hold the record for the person who has occupied the same Council house in UK for the longest period of time.

Dinky would only be a teenager when WW2 broke out in 1939. So, I'm not sure exactly when she volunteered to join the WRNS, the Women's Royal Naval Service. During this period, she met Albert Hatfield, whose family lived in the north of Hull. He would become her husband at St. Aidan's Church in 1948, after having served in the Navy during the war, sailing to many parts of Asia and the Middle East.

Dinky & Albert on their wedding day in 1948

Not long after they married, my grandfather suffered his stroke. So, Dinky and Albert stayed on at his house to look after him, with my Mum's frequent help, as we lived just two houses along the street.

Dinky and Albert were always very fond of animals, and apart from my grandfather's parrot Joey that they "inherited", they also had "Rip" a lovely black and white mongrel for many years, not to speak of several cats and other dogs later too. However, Rip was the one that taught me to like pets, as I would spend many hours playing with him in my early childhood.

As a family, we were very close to Dinky and Albert, not only because of living almost next door, but because we shared the same sort of basic human values. When necessary, I would do errands for Dinky, if she was busy or not feeling well. In regard to Albert, I would consider him to be the closest of my six uncles, as I spent a lot of time at their house with both Uncle Albert and Auntie Dinky during my early childhood. From the age of about 9 or 10, he would take me to see the "Tigers" (Hull City Football Club) at Boothferry Park (their stadium at that time) over a period of probably 5 years (see a later Chapter). Eventually, in 1957, when I was 12, their son, Steven, was born.

Peggy and Frank

Peggy was my mother's youngest sister, only 15 years older than me, having been born in 1927. As such, she was the one who did the baby-sitting for her eldest sister, when my Mum went out at night dancing with my Dad, to the theatre or to any of the Scouting and church events. As a result, we struck up a *very* close relationship and I can perfectly say that Peggy was my "closest" aunt.

Peggy and Frank on their wedding day

I have really no recollections of how Peggy met Frank McGee, whom she married on April 1st, 1950, and with whom she had 3 children (Glynis, Owen and Helene). I do remember that, recently married, they went to live over a sweet shop to the west of Hull, where I would occasionally stay overnight. Peggy would teach me to play different types of card games plus Monopoly and Cribbage, and would give me ginger beer of her own making to drink. Thus my love of anything ginger since then!

I always got on very well with Frank, who was what they called in those days a "travelling salesman". By the time I was about 12, I would accompany him some days during my summer holidays on his sweet-selling rounds in Hull to visit all sorts of shops and stores. At one time, he would take me together with his 2-year old daughter Glynis on these rounds. I would have to look after my little cousin during the time Frank would be absent from the car. I remember well that his car was a Morris Minor and probably the first car to be seen in the family. Unfortunately, he died before reaching retirement age, of a sudden heart attack in a bank when depositing money from his sales visits.

In the early 1960's, Frank's job would take the family to Sleaford (south Lincolnshire), where they lived for several years. Then he moved to Doncaster, where they bought a house and where Helene went to the Grammar School. I visited them in Sleaford, during the time when I had my own car in Britain. Then when on leave in UK from Colombia, I would always spend time (sometimes overnight) with Peggy in Doncaster on my way down from Hull to London. In fact, in April 1976, when I had a business trip to Germany, Sofia and I left our eldest son, Emlyn, just 6 months old, in Peggy's care in Doncaster for a week whilst we spent several days at the BASF HQ in Ludwigshafen.

*

NOTE: For details of the children and grandchildren of my Aunts and Uncles, please refer to the separate sheets of Family Trees that will be available for those interested.

Chapter 4

EARLY VIVID MEMORIES: WORLD WAR 2

According to my birth certificate, my parents were living at 28 Savery Street, when I was born.

28 Savery Street in 2016 (with little change over 70 + years)

With my mother at 30 Stanhope Ave.

At entrance to the Hull Kingston Rugby ground (late 1942)

I do remember, however, many mentions that my mother made of their home at 4 Telford Street (see photo in earlier chapter), just off the more residential part of Holderness Road, Kingston-upon-Hull, almost opposite the main entrance to the East Park. That must have been another house my parents rented before or after I was born until moving finally to 27 St. John's Grove (though I can only speculate on this point), where I would spend all my childhood and adolescence.

Additionally, I have just found out that the 1939 Official Register (a special Census taken around the outbreak of WW2) gives their address as 63 Telford Street, which must have been a third house they rented before moving to St. John's Grove. All three houses in Savery Street and Telford Street are in fact only about 150 to 200 metres apart, and somewhat similar in design.

Though it's very normal for anyone not to remember very much about the first five years of life, by the same token, traumatic and/or life shattering events during those early years tend to stick in one's mind for ever. So, my first vivid memories relate to a period when I would be just over 2 years old. By that time, our family had moved to the Council house just two doors away from my grandparents' house in St. John's Grove (photo below of that house today).

27 St. John's Grove, as it is today (courtesy of Google)

The war was raging and my home town, Hull (or Kingston upon Hull, as it should be called) was under constant attack from the German warplanes. As Wikipedia now tells us:

<<*Hull was the most severely damaged British city or town apart from London during the Second World War, with* **95 percent of houses damaged.** *Hull had more than 1,000 hours spent under air raid alerts. Hull was the target of the first daylight raid of the war and the last piloted air raid on Britain.*

Of a population of approximately 320,000 at the beginning of the war, approximately 152,000 were made homeless as a result of bomb destruction or damage. Overall almost 1,200 people were killed and 3,000 injured by the air raids.

More than 5,000 houses were destroyed and half of the city centre destroyed. The cost of bomb damage was estimated at £20 million (1952, £502,109,515 as a consumer price equivalent), with 3,000,000 square feet (280,000 m²) of factory space, several oil and flour mills, the Riverside Quay and 27 churches, 14 schools or hospitals, 42 pubs and 8 cinemas ruined; only 6,000 out of the 91,000 houses were undamaged at the end of the war. The extent of the damage was similar to that of the Plymouth Blitz. However, despite the damage the port continued to function throughout the war.

Large-scale attacks took place on several nights in March 1941, resulting in some 200 deaths. The most concentrated attacks were between 3 and 9 May 1941, resulting in 400 deaths and another large-scale attack took place in July 1941 with around 140 fatalities.

The city spent more than 1,000 hours under alert during raids from 19 June 1940 to 1945, with a total of over 1,200 people in the city killed as a result of the bombing. >>

*

NOTE: I have included a series of photos showing Hull's terrible bomb damage, as an Appendix to this part of my book. I also recommend the following video link which shows vivid scenes of bomb damage:

https://www.youtube.com/watch?v=s_UjFOlREgA]

From other reports I have read of events at the time, I find that in early 1943 there were air raids over Hull which could have stuck in my mind, though at the early age of just 7 or 8 months, I hardly think this possible. So, the reports of raids in late 1943 and early 1945 would presumably be the ones that created such vivid memories.

The air raid warnings would sound off with their menacing whine, calling us to scramble out of the house to the nearby air-raid shelter. We would huddle together in the shelter with several neighbours, probably up to 10 or a dozen in all. I remember very clearly the hushed wait, with few comments from anyone until we would hear in the distance the characteristic whistle of the buzz bombs announcing an imminent bombing. But where would that bomb or those bombs end up? On us as a prime target? Maybe 100 yards away? A few miles from here? Or would they be aimed at another spot much farther inland?

Later in life, when I first arrived in Colombia, I would frequently relive the experience of that air raid warning, because one of Cali's fire stations would use the same siren with the same whine to mark the time at 12 noon every day!

<<*On 24 June* [1943 – when I would be just a year old] *a larger-scale attack took place, with the city centre targeted again. During this attack the well-known Hull Municipal Museum was destroyed by fire. The government allowed Hull to be named specifically as the target of the attack and the Hull Daily Mail ran a front-page headline the next day. Another attack took place on 13/14th July, which appears have been intended to damage the railway system and caused more than 20 deaths. Two further attacks later in the year failed to penetrate the city's defences.*

No bomb fell on the city in 1944. In March 1945 the city came under ground attack with cannon shells being fired. There was an attack on 17/18 March, with fragmentation grenades being dropped. >>

[Extract from FB page "Old Hull" written by Trevor Larsen former Lord Mayor of Kingston upon Hull]

The reason other Cities lost more citizens than we did in Hull was all down to one far sighted man. His name was Leo Shultz or Sir Leo Shultz as he became. He had been informed by his relatives in Poland from where his family originated, that Germany was once again, preparing for the next war by building huge amounts of weaponry, be it for the Army, the Airforce or the German Navy with the huge amount of Submarines they were building. He convinced the Hull City Council to start the biggest Air Raid Shelter initiative in the country in preparation for what he could see was about to be unleashed on our country. It was this initiative that, despite Hull being the second most bombed City in the Country after London, saved the lives of many thousands of our citizens including myself. He had these shelters built in the gardens of most Council Houses (we had one in our garden on 40th Avenue when we moved in back in 1992!) on the end of the many terraces that Hull had back then, in the City Centre, and anywhere else the people could benefit from them being there and available. It was this single initiative that was the difference between Hull, having along with London and other Cities, a huge and bigger loss of life than we had, which was circa 2000 dead. Other less bombed Cities lost many thousands more than we lost in Hull. He eventually was Knighted and rightly so. When I first joined the Labour Party, I had the privilege of meeting him at many meetings. He was an extremely intelligent and nice man it was my honour to meet.

Apart from London, Hull was the most severely bombed British city during the Second World War. There were 86 German air raids, the first on 19 June 1940 and the last on 17 March 1945. 86,715 buildings were damaged and 95 per cent of houses were damaged or destroyed. Of a population of approximately 320,000 at the beginning of the war, approximately 152,000 were made homeless as a result of bomb destruction or damage. Almost 1,200 people were killed and 3,000 injured. Much of the city centre was completely destroyed and heavy damage was inflicted on residential areas, industry, the railways and the docks. The suffering of the people of Hull was acknowledged by Herbert Morrison, the wartime Home Secretary in his autobiography:

"But in my experience and from remembrance of the reports, I would say that the town that suffered most was Kingston-upon-Hull. ... Morning after morning the BBC reported that raiders had been over a 'north-east town'

and so there was none of the glory for Hull which known suffering might produce.

The raids on Hull were only occasionally concentrated so that the devastation of a few houses did not produce stories of disaster and heroism to repeat far and wide. Hull often suffered for what might be said to be no rhyme or reason except that it was an easy target. But it was night after night. Hull had no peace. I have since been honoured by this courageous town by being appointed High Steward and it was a privilege for me to tell the citizens that the government was fully aware of their sufferings during the war and the heroic manner in which they had endured them."

(Morrison HS. An Autobiography by Lord Morrison of Lambeth. London: Odhams Press, 1960).

Apparently it was on the direct orders of Winston Churchill not to publicise the pounding that Hull was on the receiving end of almost on a nightly basis. We received all this attention for two reasons: (1) the Convoys to supply the Russian Cities of Murmansk and Archangel were often leaving from Hull to rendezvous off the north Scottish Coast with other vessels, to form a protective Convoy; (2) When the German Bombers could not find their original clear target because of low cloud or fog, on their way back to the 'Fatherland' they would fly over Hull and drop their deadly load here rather than waste them by dropping them in the sea on their way back home. They couldn't land with them back in Germany as their Aircraft would have been far too heavy to arrive back safely. I have no Idea of Churchill's thinking regarding not to publicise the terrible damage that Hull was suffering, while allowing the air raids on these other places to be made public. It makes no sense or logic to me when he accepted the other places having their name and damage they suffered regularly broadcast on the BBC.

https://www.youtube.com/watch?v=iq_0pZ2WRqk [Video of Hull, 1930's?]

My father had wanted to "do his bit" in the war, but as a time-served carpenter, he was declared to be in a "reserved occupation" (i.e. prohibited from enlisting in the Armed Forces), and was assigned to the packing of armament on warships that left the port of Hull for the Baltic and Scandinavia. Nevertheless, he did enlist for duty in the "Specials", the special police force that did different wartime tasks locally including the manning of antiaircraft guns on the higher buildings in the city. This included the main office block of Reckitt's World Headquarters in Dansom Lane, which would have been one of the highest buildings in the city at the time.

Anti-aircraft crew

Dad in his "Specials" uniform, with Muriel in Grandma's garden

Dad in the RAF towards the end of the War

<<Attacks continued sporadically through late May, June and July, [1941] with a major attack on east Hull and the Victoria Dock on the night of 18/19 July. Reckitt's (Dansom Lane) and the East Hull gas works were also badly damaged. Around 140 people were killed by the bombing, many from the areas around the works. >>

On the night of July 18/19th, my father was thankfully **off duty**, taking a rest from his usual night-time duty of manning the anti-aircraft guns. The building was reduced to rubble by a German attack and all those on duty perished. Had it not been for this stroke of good fortune, there would have been no father, no me and definitely no "Strawberries in the Garden"!

Herein lays an amazing irony, since on the second floor of Reckitt's main office block (rebuilt, of course, after the War) I would find my first job after leaving school, as Personal Assistant to the Director for Latin America. My work in their Hull offices would last 5 ½ years and with the 7 years I served the company in Colombia would total a full 12 ½ years. This sent me half way round the world to a new life.

The video link below (with grateful thanks to Don Tellonme) was recently brought to my attention on Internet. It reinforces my memories of standing outside Paragon Station (Hull's rail terminal/interchange in the centre of town) just after the War and of being amazed at the amount of rubble almost as far as the eye could see on all sides – a really daunting sight. I recommend looking it up.
https://www.youtube.com/watch?v=xayHnW7vV5M   [Video of photos taken during the Hull Blitz]

Chapter 5

GROWING UP IN HULL WITH VARYING AILMENTS

With such a scale of damages in the city, Hull was a somewhat bleak place to live in immediately after the Second World War. Coupled with this, the first few winters after the end of the war would bring a lot of snow, bitter winds and long periods of harsh weather in general. The living conditions of many people were not at all adequate, as a result of the war damage. Houses had no overall heating apart from an open fire in the living room. Double glazing had yet to be invented, or at least adopted in Britain. In many cases, the bomb damage had not yet been repaired or had not been done effectively. So, the winters were hard to endure, and many people suffered a great deal.

Winter in Hull, late 1940's

From an early age, it seems I experienced frequent problems with my tonsils, which, over time, got progressively worse. As a consequence, at the age of about four and a half, my local GP (general practitioner), Dr. Malczewski, arranged for me to be operated on in the Hull Children's Hospital, then behind the old central Bus Station, early in 1947. Dr. Malczewski was a refugee from the war in Poland with a wonderful manner as a GP.

To this day, I remember the cold open ward, with more than 20 beds aligned along the two walls facing each other, all occupied by small children more or less of a similar age to myself. My turn came round for the tonsillectomy and I was trundled out on a stretcher to an operating room to the left, where I believe (though my memory is hazy about this) I was given a gas anaesthetic and had my tonsils taken out. When I came round, the natural pain ensued, for which the nurses would offer ice-cream, though I have a feeling that I refused it at the beginning. Eventually, I was persuaded to have at least a small portion which slowly relieved the pain and allowed me to go home a little later on that cold wintery afternoon.

View of a ward very similar to one in the Hull Children's Hospital (1940's)

A second trip to the Children's Hospital would come up not so many months later, when on my 6th Birthday, as had become the tradition in the family, I would have the privilege of picking the first batch of my father's strawberries, which he grew (with a little help from me) in our back garden, together with all sorts of other vegetables and fruit. The strawberries would always be ripe towards the end of June, coinciding with my birthday, as the climate in Hull wouldn't bring them to maturity any earlier.

On that occasion, I was carrying a very ordinary white bowl (remember, no plastics in those days), but tripped up long before I ever got near the strawberries. I fell on the stone paver path which went up the middle of our 100 foot long garden dividing it into two. The bowl smashed into many pieces under me, severing, as I fell, one of the blood vessels in my right wrist. The gash would require several stitches; so, we had to rush into the centre of town quickly (probably by taxi?), since it was a Sunday and there was no public transport to take us there. I still have the white scar line as a tribute to those strawberries to this very day.

The growing of strawberries formed an important element of summer life whilst we lived at St. John's Grove. I would take ever more interest in their growth, and look forward every year to the few weeks in Hull's climate when there would be ripe fruit to collect. Some 9 years after leaving Hull, when Sofia and I had our first house in Bogotá, I returned to growing them in our garden. There we were able to enjoy several crops throughout the year, as a result of constant climate of the high level Andean plateau. Growing strawberries has now become a hobby, an essential part of life in retirement in Dapa, though sometimes with frustratingly varying results in view of the extremes of the tropical Colombian climate.

The winter of 1948/49 was especially severe, and Southcoates Lane Primary School, where I had started at the age of 5 in 1947 was an old building with very high ceilings and rather inefficient heating, which sometimes worked and most times didn't. Also the toilets were at the end of the playground more than 50 yards away from the building itself, which in autumn and winter made for a freezing walk whenever nature required. I speculate a bit when I say the lack of my tonsils may have left me with a reduced defence mechanism, but this may well have made it easier for me to fall foul of pneumonia in that late autumn/early winter of 1948. In any case, as more events in later life have shown, I seem to have inherited a weak immune system from my Mum and Granma Gertie on the Welsh side of the family.

That year in the late winter and early spring, I became VERY ill, and spent a total of 6 weeks in bed. If it hadn't have been for the "new" antibiotic penicillin, recently introduced to the UK at that time, and all the close attention of my mother and Dr. Malczewski, I wouldn't be here today. Being still in an experimental stage, this antibiotic was only available at the time as an injection. So, my parents had to sign a formal dispensation saying that if anything adverse happened, the doctor and the recently founded NHS wouldn't be to blame.

In all, it took 21 injections to put me on the road to recovery. Dr. Malczewski would visit me daily to apply the new injection. Those were the days of regular home visits by one's GP for any manner of ailments. Eventually, I was able to return to school, after (I believe) the Easter holidays, having missed almost the whole Winter Term.

When I came to be about 9 years old, another problem would arise. I apparently consumed chewing gum quite often – a practice not that unusual for a young child at the time. However, that was blamed for a sudden blinding pain that affected me one day. Dr. Malczewski diagnosed a "grumbling appendix", which could deteriorate into a complete appendicitis at any minute. What medicine he prescribed me I am not sure (probably an antibiotic), but after several days of serious pain, the problem slowly waned and since then, I have never had any more problems with my appendix.

The pneumonia would repeat on me several years later, just after Christmas in my first year at Hull Grammar School. It was feared I might need quite a while off school (which could have affected my automatic progress to the second year), but in the end, I was only away for 3 weeks and was sent a number of lessons to do at home whilst ill, in order to keep me up-to-date with my classes.

Chapter 6

MY FIRST SCHOOL & A LONG-LASTING FRIENDSHIP

On Tuesday, September 2nd/1947, having reached the age of 5, my mother took me the few hundred yards along our street to our neighbourhood school, Southcoates Primary, where I would duly start my education. This was, and still is, a walled-in building with two entrances on the Southcoates Lane side for the Primary and Junior sections respectively. Both had internal metal railings to prevent children running out of the playground directly into the road that had and continues to have a lot of fast traffic.

Another boy, Ralph, arrived at the school by chance at the same gate at that same moment. He was slightly taller than me, and was accompanied by his very tall mother, Mrs. Oldfield, who lived a few hundred yards away from the school on Lodge Street in the other direction towards Holderness Road. The two mothers started up a conversation, and we two boys would become close friends to this very day.

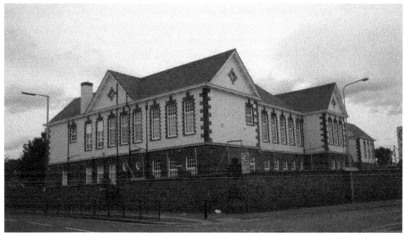

Side View of Southcoates Lane School, with the Primary Section on the Ground Floor and the Junior School above.

The primary years from the age of 5 till 8 would pass with little significance apart from my bad bout of pneumonia. In fact, what I can recall of those 3 years is very scanty, except for the fact that we had huge classes of 50 and up to 52 pupils on the school's ground floor! At the time, my friendship with Ralph was growing with fairly frequent visits to his house, which also helped me to get to know better his neighbouring friends, and our class mates, Marcia Moxon and Margaret Finney.

The Junior School part of Southcoates Primary is another story. There, at the age of 8, I was welcomed by Miss Dobson, at the time a young teacher recently graduated, I believe. She was the teacher in charge of my first junior class, who would leave a lasting impression on me as a result of her intense interest in her pupils, despite the huge classes of 50 or 52 pupils each. We would also be taught certain subjects (one was Geogtraphy) by Mr. Stephenson and Mr. Atkinson. The school's music teacher, Mr. Metcalf, played the piano for the morning "assembly" and Miss Rainer was Head of the Junior School at the time.

When I was 9 or 10 (in 1951 or 52), Mr. Metcalf persuaded me to join the school's choir, whose main objective was to form part of a city-wide young people's choir, which participated in what would become a local tradition in the 1950's and 60's at Hull's City Hall (a beautiful concert hall with one the best organs in Britain). This became the annual Combined Schools' Christmas Carol Concert, organised and directed by Mr. Metcalf himself. My participation in this event would go on till 1957, even though I had moved on to be a pupil of Hull Grammar School. I thoroughly enjoyed the two concert nights we would perform each year and was disappointed to have to leave the choir. But when the GCE exams were looming up, there was just not enough time to attend the rehearsals.

By the time the 1953 Easter holidays had come and gone, the 11+ exams were over and done with. One's secondary school destiny was sealed during those few short sessions of pen pushing and brain effort. Southcoates Junior School teachers, Mr. Stevenson, Mr. Atkinson and Miss Dobson, were all confident of a job well done.

Despite a kind of scholastic rivalry, apparently largely unperceived by my friend

Ralph, the two of us struck up a truly close personal friendship, spending time at each other's homes quite frequently over a period of 5 or 6 years, until he left Hull for Liverpool in 1955. I can even remember (or am I dreaming up this one?) that I travelled to Liverpool on one occasion and stayed with Ralph for a few days, when we were teenagers.

Ralph and I both went to the church's Sunday School, and, apart from being in the same primary school class from Monday to Friday, we also saw each other weekly at the Cubs Tuesday evening meeting, going to an annual camp at Skeffling together on one occasion.

We belonged to the Cubs (and later Scouts) at St. Aidan's Church, on Southcoates Avenue, only a couple of 100 yards from Ralph's house and less than half a mile from mine.

To this day I can vividly remember Ralph's house at 123 Lodge Street, just round the corner from our very good friends (Marcia Moxon and Margaret Finney) who lived in Telford Street, and had both attended the same primary school as us. There was a rear access "tenfoot" (alley or lane) for these houses, which effectively joined up Telford Street with Lodge Street at the back of the houses, and I would take advantage of this to make contact with all of them when I raced round on my bike on a weekend. [On a recent trip to UK in 2007, I was able to make a brief contact with Marcia by phone in the Midlands, where she apparently has lived for many years.]

In Hull, at that time, the education system at the secondary level had several "Grammar Schools", maybe one or two technical schools and a series of "secondary moderns", all of whose pupils were classified according to their results in the 11+ exams. So far as I know, there were only two private schools: Tranby's, for girls, and Hymer's, for boys. In the early 70's (I believe), this state system was reorganised, with all Hull's secondary schools being converted to the "comprehensive system". This, in very general terms, meant a levelling **down** of the education standards, with absolutely no way of providing for the more capable (above average) students – a real tragedy for the progress of the city in the future.

Ralph was often pushing me out of the first place in the pupil rankings at the end of each term at Southcoates Junior School. However, the school entered us both for the Hymer's College Governors' Scholarship exams. Everyone, especially my parents, said I could make the grade and I was told that I was the one who would be successful (most probably they said the same to Ralph), but in the end, he was the one who got a place there. Whether we actually were given the results of these exams, I don't remember.

I awoke rather early that Saturday morning, (whether in late May or early June of 1953, I quite forget now) ready to catch a bus into Hull's central bus station, and then a second one to the Hymer's school lane. My mother went with me, as Dad must have been working, and we finally reached that hallowed entrance, all very posh! What an amazing difference from the school I had known those past 6 years – a well kept building, though not too new, but with an air of sophistication I had never experienced before. Not at all like that old, almost decrepit building on Southcoates Lane, where the heating didn't always work, the toilets were a total shame and the pupils crammed into large rooms with high ceilings and roofs and more than 50 per class! However, all this was compensated for by the dedication and personal warmth of the wonderful teachers at Southcoates Primary.

Almost 60 years later would I learn that neither of us (Ralph or I) had in fact secured a place at Hymer's as a result of those exams that we had worked so hard for. However Hymer's College was a direct grant school and, as such, was obliged to provide a significant number (maybe 25 to 30) of 'free' places to pupils from the local education authority based on their marks in the normal eleven plus examination. So, it was this way in which Ralph entered Hymer's.

Chapter 7

PRIMARY SCHOOL AND LAZZARINI'S

When I was between 18 and 24 months old, my parents had moved from a privately rented house at No.28 Savery Street in East Hull not all that far away to a Council House at 27 St. John's Grove, just 2 doors (houses) away from my grandparents, the Mills. This meant that the primary and junior school, on Southcoates Lane that I would attend, was, very conveniently, just two hundred yards from our house.

At first, during a good part of the first two years, my mother would take me to school in the morning, collect me at midday, take me back at 1:30 or 2pm. and wait for me again at 4pm. to take me home. However, before the second year finished, I would walk and, more often, run on my own the few yards to and from school.

As I got used to my new school, I also started to explore the shops that stood on the other side of Southcoates Lane, opposite our school, crossing the road with the kind guidance of the "lollipop" man. The principal attraction of these shops was the one directly in front of the main entrance to the school: Lazzarini's. It was a shop which sold all sorts of chocolates, sweets, ice-cream and any related snacks – pure heaven for a little boy. Once I began to receive "pocket money" around the age of 7, I would initially spend most of this on different types of chocolate and sweets at 4pm. immediately after the end of the school day.

Over the space of 12 to 15 years of regular (sometimes daily) visits to this shop, I would get to know the owners very well, especially Peter Lazzarini, their eldest son. However, it would seem that in the late 1970's or 80's, when the area of shops on Southcoates Lane became extremely depressed with the advent of large supermarkets, the Lazzarinis must have sold their business, as nowadays on Google one can see its premises are occupied by a Mexican Takeaway.

As I lived so close to my school, I soon made friends with several other pupils (apart from Ralph Oldfield) who lived equally near. One was Gordon Lawtey, in Edgware Avenue, a short cul-de-sac opposite my school. He had a big model railway set and often invited me to run it at his house. His family would also invite me on two or three occasions to spend a weekend with them at a caravan they owned on the edge of the cliffs at Aldborough.

Others with whom I was fairly friendly at the time were Gordon Wright, Clive Singleton, Ian Deutsch, Margaret Finney, Marcia Moxon, John Pawson, Raymond Crossland and Lyn Proctor. Later on, through contacts in the Scouts, I would be also become friends with Chris East (still a contact on Skype) and Bruce Leng, who eventually devoted his life to the Anglican Church as a clergyman.

Chapter 8

CUB CAMPS AND CHILDHOOD ADVENTURES

As I mention in another chapter, from the age of 5 or 6, since my Auntie Vera was the Akela (adult leader) of St. Aidan's Cub Pack, I was adopted as their "mascot". I would also accompany the Cubs to their annual 4-day summer camp on a farm owned by a Mr. Medforth at Skeffling, near Easington, just 9 miles (14 kms.) before reaching Spurn Point to the east of Hull.

When I look at a map these days, I always wonder why such a potentially bleak place should have been chosen for a group of boys from 8 to 10 years old! Nevertheless, a good time was usually had by all at the 3 or 4 camps I attended, especially as the farmer was a wonderful man, who even put us up in a barn with straw for beds on one occasion when we suffered very bad weather. On another occasion, there was an "event" that many of us will never forget.

Off we go to Cub Camp on the back of a lorry (probably 1953)!

One summer, probably of 1952, when I was 10, the recently appointed young curate from our church (St. Aidan's), Rev. Roger Robinson, decided to pay a visit to "his" Cub Pack at their annual camp together with his fiancée or new wife (I don't now recall whether he had already married by then). How exactly he would have travelled there, I'm not sure, since at that time, I don't think he would have had a car. However, I do remember it was one of the hottest summer camps I would ever attend (several of them were total washouts!).

It was a wonderful sunny day. Suddenly, only minutes after the curate arrived at the farmhouse, there was a lot of shouting, some laughter and much embarrassment, as Rev. Robinson had been stung by a bee, right on the top of his nose! Within minutes his nose became dark red and very swollen. I have no idea what exactly was done to relieve his pain and suffering, presumably at the farmhouse, as he was not seen again that day at the camp. But he did survive.

Rev. Robinson would stay on at St. Aidan's to be probably the most cherished vicar the church has ever had. I am proud to have been able to correspond with him until his death last year (2016), at the age of 92. For several years he had been living in an old people's home in Leeds, and still occasionally preached locally.

Chapter 9

Holidays at Bridlington

Around the summer of 1947 or maybe 48, my Dad decided that the family would enjoy a week's summer holiday at the local seaside resort (as they were then called) of Bridlington. If my memory serves me right, No. 44 Marine Drive, overlooking the Promenade was called the Bellevue or Belview Guest House at the time. From what I see in Google, it has now been turned into the Royal Court Apartments, along with adjoining properties. It was a cosy place with good clean bedrooms, a bathroom for use by two or three rooms on the same floor (a normal arrangement in those days), and a dining room downstairs, with some really fine food, which we always seemed to give us no end of pleasure.

I have the idea that we stayed at this guest house for at least 4 or 5 summers, spending good times on the beach (just across the road from the guest house), visiting the shops and entertainment arcades, and going to see shows, several of which were presented at that time in the Bridlington Spa, only about 100 yards from the guest house. We would sometimes also take a ride up the coast on buses or trains to Flamborough, Filey or even Scarborough to explore the tourist spots there.

When I look back on these holidays, I can only wonder how my father could have afforded to take us there on his foreman joiner's wages at the time (about £2 per week). However, every year it was a firm aim of his to give the family a week's rest away from Hull, in what was then a reasonably priced, but good quality lodging house next to the beach, whatever that might have cost him.

On one of these holidays, probably in 1949, when strolling along the Bridlington Promenade with my parents only a few yards from the guest house, we would pass by a boating pool, where families hired boats to take their children for rides on the water. It was hardly more than 100 yards long and only some 10 or 15 yards wide. I see from Google that the pool still exists, though whether it has any boats for children's rides, I would seriously doubt.

I must have been idling behind my parents on that occasion and stopping to see who knows what, when, "plop", I fell into the pool, maybe headfirst without my parents noticing me. The pool was quite a lot deeper than one would have imagined; so a 7-year old boy, no more than 3 foot (1 metre) tall, dropped right to the bottom of the pool. I came up again in panic, maybe once or probably twice, until my parents realised what was happening and pulled me out dripping wet. I always blame this serious incident for my inability to learn to swim, as I could never afterwards get the hang of being able to float.

On holiday at Bridlington – late 1940's

Other childhood "adventures" of mine included the few trips I would make to Aldborough, only about 12 miles east of Hull on the coast. As I mentioned earlier, I would be invited there by the parents of Gordon Lawtey (a slightly plump primary school friend) to the caravan they owned at the edge of the cliffs at Aldborough. The caravan was fairly small and one couldn't say it was too cosy, but I spent several good days there together with Gordon. How we would do the journey, I now don't recall, as I don't think Gordon's father had a vehicle. Even at that period, the caravan had to be moved slightly inland every two or three years, as whole sections of the cliffs would regularly collapse into the sea and leave the caravan teetering on the edge, with the danger of taking them with it!

Chapter 10

CHRISTMAS (AND NEW YEAR) IN THE PRITCHETT FAMILY

CHRISTMAS

Not long after Grandad Harold had died, (maybe in December 1946), when my Uncles and Aunts had returned some time before from their duties in the armed forces both in England and abroad, Grandma Alice (Pritchett) organised what would be my first Christmas family gathering at her home, when all four families on my father's side would be present.

These Christmas "parties" usually took place on Boxing Day (December 26th.) every year, as each family would have their own Christmas dinner on 25th at their respective homes. Sometimes we were accompanied by one or more of my father's aunts (Aunt Lizzie or Auntie Gertie) and I seem to remember that some family members on my mother's side (especially Dinky and Albert and maybe Peggy and Frank) were with us on several occasions after marrying. So, we would end up with probably 12 or 15 family members plus an ever increasing number of cousins, as the years went by. I attended all these gatherings until the Christmas of 1965 (a few months before I left for Colombia) but they would continue in 1966 and 1967 in my absence, until my grandmother Alice died in early 1968. The family would gather for a late lunch, with Grandma Pritchett preparing, in the earlier years, the main part with different cold meats, pork pies and their trimmings, and each family would bring with them additional dishes, both savoury and sweet, many of them desserts. If my memory is correct, Auntie Muriel would almost always do a batch of wonderful mince pies. We would all have a good chat for several hours well into the evening, since this was the main occasion in the year that we would all meet up at the same time.

Sometimes, one of my aunts (again usually Muriel) would organise a rowdy game for us all to play, more than anything to keep the younger cousins occupied.

Then, after 6pm or 7pm, each of the families would start to make their way home, by foot or by bus in the 1940's and 50's, often through the snow, to our different homes, which were between a mile and 4 miles from Grandma's house. Not until the early 60's would any of the families have a car.

One memory that was almost escaping me was of the years when at these Christmas gatherings we would roast chestnuts on Grandma's open coal fire. What a wonderful experience for all us young cousins to see the chestnuts roasting in the red coals and what a wonderful flavour they always had when done! It makes me wonder where all the chestnuts in England have gone. I haven't seen them in England for years! So far as I know, you don't find them easily these days, whereas in Italy they have conserved this tradition and even have an annual chestnut festival.

Chestnuts, like the ones we would roast at Christmas

In my first 6 years in Colombia, as a bachelor, I would miss these family gatherings. My Christmases would be spent with friends from the British community. However, in December 1973, I made it back to UK for Christmas to coincide with my father's wedding to Joyce on December 30th. that year. My memory is hazy, but I'm sure we had a family gathering on that occasion.

After my marriage, Sofia and I renewed this Christmas tradition, first inviting a few friends (in Bogota in 1974), and later with the children and Sofia's family in Cali. We are proud to see that our children are continuing with the tradition, which nowadays implies gathering the family together from several different countries and continents. They try to choose a new venue each time we meet, so that we can all get to know as many countries as possible. After gathering in northern France on a non-Christmas date, we have spent Christmas together since in Salobreña (Spain) and recently in Punta Cana (Dominican Republic). This last year (2016) we gathered in Dapa, but as Melissa was pregnant with Hannah, she, Luivi and Bianca were unable to join up with us.

New Year

January 1st, 1973 was the first time that New Year's Day had been declared a public holiday in England and Wales, the very same day that the UK became a full member of the European Economic Community (EEC), as it was called at that time. That was several years after I had left Britain to live in Colombia. Therefore, during the 23 years that I spent in UK, it was "work as usual" on January 1st!

As I was an active member of our local church in the years I spent in Hull, the family tradition on New Year's Eve was to attend the midnight communion (mass) at 11pm. on 31st December. The service would finish a few minutes before midnight. Then, on leaving the church, all those attending would wish each other a "Happy New Year" and make their way home in the snow (mostly) in the first few minutes of the New Year. Until 1973, there had **never** been any tradition of formal New Year celebrations in England.

Paragon Station, Hull, 1950's

Chapter 11

ADVENTURES IN KENT & LONDON

Those holidays in Bridlington that I described would only occupy one of the six weeks of school holidays that I and all children of school age would have every summer. Additionally, and partly to keep me well occupied, my mother arranged for me to travel down to London to stay in West Wickham, Kent, with her Auntie Annie, who was the sister of my Welsh grandmother. In this way, I was encouraged to acquire a broader view of the world (or at least of my own country), which was the way my parents saw it at the time. These adventures started when I was probably 7 or 8, and when I say "adventure", for me it was really that.

On the first occasion, I was taken to Paragon Station, Hull's rail departure terminal or Interchange (as they now call it), where, after buying me a ticket for King's Cross Station (London), my parents entrusted me, together with my case and packed lunch, to the first amiable looking lady they found in the third class carriage!

Between three and a half and four hours later, my train emerged from the entrance tunnel at King's Cross, to glide into the platform, where I was duly being met by Auntie Annie and Uncle George Miller. From there, they would take me to their home at 64 Glebe Way, in West Wickham, Kent on a suburban train which left from another of the big London terminals, Charing Cross.

Auntie Annie, my mother's aunt, was an unassuming lady with a lovely melodious Welsh accent, and a really caring way about her. Uncle George, her husband, was a high-ranking Civil Servant, the Head of the government's Estate Duty Office at the time, a very responsible government position in the centre of London. However, he was a very amiable person and went out of his way to take care of me. He would take time off from the office to do the rounds with me of all the main Museums in London and also the London Zoo, sometimes accompanied by Auntie Annie, sometimes just the two of us together – a really wonderful experience.

Auntie Annie & Uncle George with
son Kenneth & daughter Dolly

Auntie Annie & Uncle George's House,
West Wickham

I stayed with them on each occasion for maybe two weeks (it seemed an age to me), learning to get on with Auntie Annie's lovely ginger cats (three, I believe), enjoying the fire station just across the road from their house, occasionally helping her to bake cakes and tarts, getting to know my way about the shops in the two main shopping streets of West Wickham and riding back and forth to central London on the commuter trains and the Tube. I would also get to know their daughter, Auntie Dolly, who, not much after my first visit, would marry Arthur Houghton (a northerner). After marrying they stayed on at the Glebe Way house to live as a couple, but never had any children.

These visits to West Wickham would be repeated, mostly on my own, though once with my Mum, until my father got his first car (probably in 1955?). That year he duly drove us all down to Kent, instead of making the annual trip to Bridlington. We stopped at several places on the way, including Coventry Cathedral and the Bekonscot Model Village & Railway, a miniature replica of many famous British tourist sites and villages, near Beaconsfield, which I remember so well to this day. After this, we stayed with the Millers in West Wickham for a few days, spending several of them doing tourism in Central London.

View of part of the Bekonscot Model Village, a mini replica of many British tourist sites

In my teenage days, I would take the train down to London and West Wickham on my own in the summer. I would have saved up part of my pocket money in prior months and would ride into Central London on the commuter train several days during my two weeks there, armed with a packed lunch, a Tube map, a street map and leaflets about the museums and other places I was aiming to visit. Thus, at a fairly early age, I came to learn a lot about all the London tourist sites, about my grandfather's birthplace, and about how to find my way around Central London and the Tube.

I would sometimes get very absorbed in the museum or special site I decided to visit on any particular day. This would mean I would have to run all the way back to the Tube station to catch the appropriate train to connect at Charring Cross with the commuter trains. The trains to West Wickham would be leaving every 10 or 15 minutes in the peak hours, but only every half hour thereafter. So, if I missed out on those earlier trains, it would mean I would arrive back at Auntie Annie's house very late and receive a firm scolding!

Chapter 12

SHOPPING FOR THE FAMILY FROM AN EARLY AGE

Around the time when I would have reached the age of 8, my mother was suffering quite a lot with problems relating to her lungs. She would appear to have chronic bronchitis, but specialists who saw her would treat her for this and similar ailments with absolutely no success. Her lungs would constantly fill with liquid, thus making her breathing extremely difficult.

This meant that, for long periods, she would feel very weak and lacking energy. So, as my father still worked on Saturdays till midday in the early 50's, it was suggested that I could help out by doing the weekly shopping for our house. This implied walking about 300 yards to our nearest shops on Southcoates Lane, where it turns south at the start of Preston Road.

Here, one then found about 20 different shops, including a Post Office branch, two bakers (one was Mrs. Mackenzie's), two food stores (one with a delicatessen), a newsagent (Ryder's) with a barber's shop at the rear, two fish and chip shops, a sweet shop (Lazzarini's), two butchers (one was Wilson's), an Ironmonger (at one time Mallory's and then Brooke's), a bicycle store, a toy shop (Birche's), a haberdashery (Mrs. Barnet's), Hastie's pharmacy (a chemist as we called it then), a shoe repairer, two greengrocers, and a Zernie's Dry Cleaners. *(See photo below of shops as in 2014)*

Courtesy of Google Maps

At first, this task was a little difficult for one so relatively young, and I would have to do several trips to the shops with my shopping list throughout the Saturday morning, in order to be able to carry the amount of groceries and other items that we would need each week. Wartime rationing of all sorts of food and other articles was still in force. So, I also had to learn about the different coupons I needed to hand over for many of the items I would buy.

The Saturday shopping expeditions continued on for many years, and I became quite an expert on how to make the money go further, what food to buy, the different types of bread, ham, meat and some of the vegetables the family would require. What I didn't have to buy very much were the fruit and "greens", since twice a week, Waudby's van would come to our home to supply all we needed in fresh produce. Most certainly these tasks had a great influence in my choice of the marketing work I would carry out later in life.

In September of 1953 when I was 11, I started the secondary school. The school's fine brand new building on Bishop Alcock Road (now demolished I understand) was at least 5 miles away from our house. So, towards the end of my first year, my parents bought me a bicycle to be able to do this journey more easily.

On the bus the journey took well over an hour and sometimes nearer two, when there was bad weather or traffic congestion. This was because one had first to take the No.45 bus into the centre of town, and then take the No.14 right up to its terminus out to the west of the city on Bricknell Avenue. However, on a bicycle, one didn't have to go through the city centre, but could do a detour via Southcoates Lane, Laburnum Avenue, Chamberlain Road, Stoneferry Bridge, Clough Road and Cottingham Road, which only took half an hour.

As a bonus, with the help of the bicycle from then onwards, I could do the shopping more easily. This would allow me to load up more bags for each journey. Or if there was a lot to buy, then the trip back home to unload and back again to the shops would be very quick, taking only a few minutes. This arrangement went on until the family left St. John's Grove for Bellfield Avenue in 1963.

Chapter 13

HOBBIES: STAMP COLLECTING, CYCLING AND BELL RINGING

From a very early age, maybe 5 or 6, I remember that stamp collecting was "all the rage". I soon acquired my first album, which I received almost certainly as a birthday present. I would hoard all and any stamps that came to our home, plus those that I would buy with part of my pocket money and others I would exchange with friends at school. Apart from this, my father's Uncle Syd, who was what one might call a professional stamp collector, would regularly send me in the post (from Barnet, London, where he lived) small packets of stamps to supplement my collection. Over a space of probably 12 to 15 years, I built up an album with more than 2,000 stamps.

Eventually, around the time when I went to live in Spain for 6 months, Uncle Syd offered to "organise" my collection, which by then had become totally chaotic in the same original album, now rather old and tatty. When I arrived back home from Spain, I found a brand new album, as a gift from Uncle Syd, amazingly well classified, with a wonderful dedication. The album, which I conserve intact to this day, is in virtually the same condition as when Uncle Syd prepared it for me more than 50 years ago. Will any of our offspring or grandchildren be interested in the album in the future? It's there for whoever wants to take a genuine interest, concentrating on stamps from the late 19th Century, and the first half of the 20th Century.

Stamp collecting, as a hobby, covered not only my childhood but also all my adolescence. However, at the time when I went to the secondary school and started to acquire experience with my bicycle, an Assistant Scout Master called George Ripon joined the St. Aidan's Scout Troop. He was a keen cyclist, and by the time I was 14, he had formed a Cycling Club, as part of additional activities for members of the Scout Troop. The aim was to cycle in a group to nearby places of interest, mainly to keep us fit, or just simply for pleasure.

At first, I would join the group for short rides, to places like Beverley, Paull and Skidby. However, as I got used to the effort that would require, I would venture on longer rides to Hornsea, Withernsea and Bridlington, up to 30 miles at a time for both the outward and the return journeys. Fortunately the traffic in the 1950's was nowhere near what it is today. So, there was little danger for 8 or 10 cyclists to be riding in a group. This activity, which of course was mainly limited to the summer months, lasted for about 3 or 4 years... until I became a bell ringer!

The very genial and popular vicar of St. Aidan's Church, Rev. Roger Robinson, saw his church in great demand for weddings in the second half of the 1950's. The children born to newlywed couples who had moved to the Preston Road estate in the 1920's and 30's had now reached marrying age. He had the bright idea to have the church's single bell tolled to advise people waiting outside the church of the moment when the happy couple would emerge as husband and wife. So, when I was about 15, he approached me to see if I was interested in taking the post of official Bell Ringer for all weddings held there.

This was quite a "responsibility", since most Saturdays (the only day weddings were held at St. Aidan's and most churches) there would be up to 5 weddings filling the whole afternoon! The task held a "compensation" of 1/6d. per wedding. That was one shilling and sixpence or what now is 7½ pence of decimal money (for those who are not familiar with Britain's old money). This formed an important addition to my weekly pocket money at the time, allowing me to buy many things for my bike, go occasionally to the cinema and to do things I hadn't even dreamt of before, including the editing of a monthly news bulletin for the Scout Group, called "Impact".

Chapter 14

LANGUAGES APPEAR AT AN EARLY STAGE TO STEER THE COURSE OF MY LIFE

Cardiff, where my mother was born, is the capital city of Wales and a port on the River Severn, at the very southern limit of the country. English was and is spoken in that area almost exclusively. On the other hand, in the northern half of Wales, many of the population speak (or at least in the early and mid twentieth century spoke) Welsh as their mother tongue.

In 1890, following the Education Act of 1870 of the British Parliament which introduced compulsory education in Wales, the Government made a concession and paid capitation grants to schools which taught Welsh. This by no means obliged any school to teach Welsh – the Act followed the English model – but it did mean that, for the first time, the Welsh language gained a toehold in the education system. So, when my mother entered the secondary school in 1921 or 22, she started to receive Welsh language classes.

However, only a year or so afterwards, when my grandfather left the sea, he was transferred with the Blue Funnel Line to the port of Hull in the north-east of England. Thus, my mother never had the chance of acquiring a deep knowledge of the Welsh language with these classes. Nevertheless, it emerged that she would retain her elementary knowledge of more than a handful of Welsh words for many years until well after I was born in 1942.

Then, when I was around 4 or 5, she started to teach me the few words that had stuck in her mind, words that I, as her pupil, still remember to this very day, such as:

1 un (een)
2 dau (die) (m); dwy (doo-ey) (f)
3 tri (tree) (m); tair (tire) (f)

4	pedwar (PED-war) (m)
5	pump (pimp)
6	chwech (ch'way'ch or ch'way)
7	saith (scyth)
8	wyth (oo-ith)
9	naw (now)
10	deg (day-g or deng)

Bread and Butter – Bara ymenyn
Red house – Ti coch

In later life, I have become convinced that my mother's "introduction" to a foreign language, however small and limited it had been, was my golden passage to start learning French with relative ease at the age of eleven on entering the secondary school. In the same way, Spanish followed two years later and subsequently guided the destiny of my whole life ever since.

This third event in the sequence of language learning (Spanish classes) began in 1955 – another accident of destiny brought about by being "in the right place at the right time", nothing more. Or maybe there were deeper forces behind all this?

When I started the secondary school at Hull Grammar School (HGS) in September 1953, I found that each school year had a total of about 120 pupils, divided into four classes of 30 pupils each (A, B, C & D streams). I must admit to being a little disappointed to find I had been assigned to the B stream, (most probably the outcome of my 11+ exams results). The only option for languages in this stream was French, whose teacher was Mr. Matthews. In contrast, the A stream was given French, German and Latin.

Not long before our second year was due to finish, a circular was handed out to all pupils in the B, C & D streams, advising us that at the start of our third year (September 1955) one of the other French teachers (Mr. "Mad Alf" Jackson, who I later learnt was the Head of Modern Languages) would be starting an "experiment" of teaching Spanish to the best 15 or 20 pupils in the French classes from these three streams precisely in our year.

I took this circular home to my parents, but long before I reached home, I had made my own decision – that I was not going to miss the opportunity of being one of those pupils taking the "experiment". **On hindsight, this can be considered as *the* decision of my life.** As my results in French had been good in these first two years at HGS, I was determined to be included in the group, for no other reason than my own personal inclination for languages.

My daughter Melissa & Granddaughter Bianca
on their first visit to Wales

Chapter 15

FATHER'S PASSIONATE DEDICATION TO THE SCOUTS PLUS A CANADIAN JAMBOREE

My father was born just two years after the Boy Scouts Association was founded in England by Robert Baden-Powell, and by the time he was of an age to join, it was an increasingly large phenomenon in Britain and several other countries. So, it wasn't surprising that he should become passionate about its principles and teachings at a time when memories of the First World War were still fresh, the world was tackling a deep economic recession and the Nazi regime was gaining strength in Germany.

Having got deeply involved in the Scouts, first at St. Columbas' Church and then with the organisation of a Group at St. Aidan's, Dad modelled his whole life on the Scouting principles of honesty, public service, classlessness, sobriety and religious adhesion.

In the mid 1950's, my father's life saw two radical changes. From overseeing carpentry jobs for many years as a Joinery Foreman, he progressed to being a Builder's Manager in his work. In the Scouts, he not only kept organising the St. Aidan's Group activities, but he went on to become District Commissioner for South East Hull, with responsibility for a total of (I think) 12 Groups.

Then, in August 1955, Dad made his first trip abroad, to Canada, where he attended the 8th World Scout Jamboree at Niagara-on-the–Lake, Ontario in Canada, together with more than 11,000 Scouts from all over the world. This was held just 14 miles north of Niagara Falls, on the banks of Lake Ontario. I remember that we were raising funds for the journey from the beginning of that year, and eventually a small group of the South East Hull Scouts would accompany my father on this epic voyage.

A final high point with his Scouting work came when Dad was awarded the Silver Acorn for his long outstanding services to Scouting, an award which he received from the hands of the Queen in London.

However, the publication of **The Chief Scouts' Advance Party Report** in 1967 introduced major changes to the Scout Association's name, uniform, sections and programme. It also recommended an age limit for different leaders to be fixed in the following years. So far as I know, this was eventually placed at 60 for District Commissioners, at a time when my father was only a few years away from this age.

Harold had widowed unexpectedly at the age of 54, shortly earlier, and now this upheaval in the Scout movement was a disheartening fact to face after devoting more than 40 years of his life to this cause. At a moment when he still considered himself in the prime of life, I am told that Dad began to feel his world was falling apart. So, when the time came to retire from the Scouts, he urgently needed another charitable "interest" to occupy his evenings and not find himself in an empty house alone with little to do.

I am not sure how the news reached Dad, but around the time when he would be relinquishing his role as Scout Commissioner in 1972, he was to hear that the Spastics Society (now known as "Scope") Hull branch was looking for a new

Leader to organise their local activities. My father applied for this position and was welcomed with open arms. I will leave this part of my story here, since the sequel forms a whole new chapter on my father's life thereafter. Needless to say, his whole world came together again.

New Theatre, Hull   H.1049

New Theatre in Hull as it was in the 1950's

Chapter 16

MOTHER'S LEGACY: THE THEATRE, FILMS, CONCERT CLASSICS AND GIGLI

My parents were very fond of their nights out, going to the theatre, to music concerts or to a dance hall. My birth, after 5 years of their marriage, didn't seem to deter them at all from keeping up with their weekly entertainment, since they would recruit as their baby sitter Doris's youngest sister (Auntie Peggy), who was just 15 years old when I was born.

As a result, it was just quite natural that my mother would begin to take me to Hull's New Theatre with her around the age of 8 or 9. Dad would come along with us on occasions, but didn't always manage to dodge his Scouting commitments. Musical comedy was Mum's favourite genre; so, over several years, I would enjoy *"Annie get your gun"*, *"Carousel"*, *"South Pacific"*, *"West Side Story"*, *"Showboat"*, *"The Desert Song"*, *"Fiddler on the Roof"*, *"Hello, Dolly"*, *"Cabaret"*, *"My Fair Lady"*, *"Oklahoma"*, *"The King & I"*, *"Oliver"*, *"Kiss me Kate"*, *"There's no Business like Show Business"*, *"The Merry Widow"*, *"The Sound of Music"* plus operettas like *"The Merry Widow"* and many others I can't now bring to mind.

I was also taken to several classical music concerts offered by the few famous artists who would manage to include Hull in their tours. The high point of this cultural immersion was when I attended the unique concert given by BENIAMINO GIGLI in the Hull City Hall on April 9th, 1952. He was the top Italian tenor of his time, reigning supreme in the early post-war years, successor to Caruso and predecessor of Pavarotti. As Wikipedia says:

<<Beniamino Gigli (March 20, 1890 – November 30, 1957) was an Italian opera singer. The most famous tenor of his generation, he was renowned internationally for the great beauty of his voice and the soundness of his vocal technique. Music critics sometimes took him to task, however, for what was perceived to be the over-emotionalism of his interpretations. Nevertheless, such was Gigli's

talent, he is considered to be one of the very finest tenors in the recorded history of music. >>

Even for a young boy of just under 10 years old, it was impressive to be a witness to such a fine performance, with Gigli's amazing voice giving magnificent interpretations of arias and some lighter songs from 7pm till well after 10pm, with only one short break of 15 minutes. I was and have been ever since so grateful and very proud to have had such a wonderful experience that I remember it as if it were yesterday. By that time, I had been in a choir for little more than a year, but, true to our Welsh heritage, I was fond of singing and learning to appreciate such a magnificent voice.

I was also taken sporadically to see films, mostly to our local Royalty cinema, only half a mile from home, though occasionally to the Regal in the centre of town, or the Savoy or the Gaumont on Holderness Road. The first two films I saw were *"The Wizard of Oz"* and *"Alice in Wonderland"* (the original version), probably at the age of 5 or 6, when I would also see a newsreel of the Queen Elizabeth II's wedding.

A few years later (maybe in 1952), my mother found that there was a presentation of "How Green was my Valley", a 1941 drama film which portrays the sentiment of the Welsh people of the South Wales Valleys, when they are faced with the building of a reservoir in one valley which will displace a lot of people from their traditional roles and villages. At that same time the exploitation of the many local coal mines was destroying the local environment. It was a very emotional characterisation of the Welsh spirit and has stayed in my mind ever since. This definitely reinforced my sense of "Welshness", stemming from my mother's family.

<< How Green Was My Valley is a 1941 drama film directed by John Ford. The movie, based on the 1939 Richard Llewellyn novel of the same name, was produced by Darryl F. Zanuck and scripted by Philip Dunne. The movie features Walter Pidgeon, Maureen O'Hara, Anna Lee, Donald Crisp, and Roddy McDowall. It was nominated for ten Academy Awards,[3] winning five, including Best Picture, Best Director and Best Cinematography and Best Supporting Actor.

The movie tells of the Morgans, a hard-working Welsh mining family living in the heart of the South Wales Valleys during the 19th century. The story chronicles life in the South Wales coalfields, the loss of that way of life and its effects on the family. The fictional village in the movie is based on Gilfach Goch;[4] Llewellyn spent many summers there visiting his grandfather, and it served as the inspiration for the novel.[5] During 1990, the movie was selected for preservation in the United States National Film Registry of the Library of Congress as being "culturally, historically, or aesthetically significant". The Academy Film Archive preserved How Green Was My Valley during 1998.[6] >>

(an extract from Wikipedia)

Not too long after (probably when I was about 12 or 13), my mother also took me to see another even stronger drama film based in Haiti. This presented the essence of Voodoo and its great influence on Haitian life, plus the consequences that arose when people got too involved with it. I'm not now sure of the title of the film, but it was quite a horrific representation of the adverse effect of Voodoo on the everyday life of the Haitians and those foreigners who came into contact with the practice. That, for certain, was the main reason for me remembering it so vividly ever since.

*One of my mother's best portraits
(late 1930's)*

Chapter 17

LONG HAUL ON THE DENTAL FRONT

My parents became very anxious when I was around the age of 10 or 11, as I had developed a "reverse bite" (upper teeth behind the lower ones) when my adult teeth appeared, because of an extremely small upper pallet. Over a period of two years, my mother would arrange appointments for me with a series of private dentists, all of whom would declare themselves unqualified or unable to take on my case and give me a normal bite.

Finally, by the time I had reached 13, she arranged for me to be seen by one of the NHS dentists in the centre of Hull. As he was one of the main representatives of the public dental service for children in the city, he had a mandate to help any child, no matter what his/her problem might be. Although we had no real references on his work, I was entrusted to this dentist (poor fellow) to correct all the defects he might find in my mouth!

His first task was to "open up" my upper pallet! This consisted in fixing me an apparatus with a central mechanism which would push parts of my pallet and my teeth outward in order to widen its size and allow the front teeth to situate themselves in front of the lower ones instead of being behind. For at least the first two years, during each of my two weekly appointments, he would insert a key which would very slowly open up the apparatus to give all the upper teeth much more room and separate some which were on top of each other. At times, it would feel as if my pallet were to crack open like a piece of rock! But eventually, with great perseverance on both sides, the task was accomplished.

At the same time, this unfortunate dentist would have to do a lot of work on my caries, since the higgledy piggledy way in which my teeth had formed, had provoked a lot of deterioration. This whole process of improving my teeth lasted for no less than 5 years, normally with appointments every two or three weeks, year in year out. Although no-one could consider that this dentist did an excellent job, at least he achieved a reasonable solution for me, through sheer determination, with some of his fillings lasting to this very day!

Chapter 18

UP THE TIGERS!

From about the age of 9 or 10, my Uncle Albert gave me the opportunity to accompany him on a Saturday afternoon to Boothferry Park, the stadium where Hull City Football Club (The Tigers) played their matches in what was then the Second Division. He was a very keen football fan and did himself play in some amateur teams in Hull over a period of several years. He would go to see "his team" (the Tigers) probably at the majority of their home matches, and would invite me to join him maybe once a month, starting in 1952, I recall.

As I was still not all that tall, I would have to take a stool with me to stand on, so that I could see the game better from the general "stands" where we would be. Those days, only a very small part of each stadium would have seats, with the rest of the fans standing throughout the whole match. This meant that a little boy like me would have little chance to see anything of the game without my stool over the heads of the adults in front.

Boothferry Park, the Tigers' first stadium, 1970's

At that time, I remember that the Tigers were sometimes in the Second Division and in one season even in the Third Division of the English Football League. Even so, the attendance at their matches would usually be over 20,000 fans and sometimes in the 30,000s. On one occasion, I do recall that an important FA Cup match with one of the "famous" teams (from what was then the First Division) drew a full capacity crowd of 55,000 people.

An ironical recollection comes to mind regarding one of the more exceptional players Hull City had in those days. He was Neil Franklin, centre-half, who, as a Stoke City player, had earned fame as an outstanding member of the England squad in the late 1940's. Hull City made a bid for him for the 1950/51 season, but he suddenly announced a move to Bogotá, Colombia, where he joined the fairly new club called Independiente Santa Fe in the local league outlawed by the incipient FIFA. The club was accused of paying "exorbitant" salaries, thereby unfairly "poaching" players from European teams!

However, it seems Neil's wife found it difficult to settle into the local culture in Bogotá. Additionally, Neil was purported to have broken a leg there and returned to UK within months of leaving. He finally joined Hull City in 1951 for 5 years. However, I was witness to the fact that he was never again the "brilliant player" he had been before his stay in Colombia, and went slowly downhill in the late 1950's. Little would I imagine that I would be hearing daily news about the club Independiente Santa Fe team in my later life!

An intriguing twist on this part of early life occurred in March 2017. By coincidence, our son Dylan, as part of a business deal, acquired the partial use of one of the special spectator boxes at the Leicester City stadium, which is less than an hour from where he lives in Northamptonshire. Leicester surprisingly took the Premier League championship in the 2015/16 season at the same time as Hull City was once again promoted to the Premier League. So, our son Dylan invited Steven (the son of my Uncle Albert) together with his daughter Megan, to accompany him to the match between the two clubs which took place on March 4th, 2017. Emlyn also was able to join the group. So, this event was a fitting moment to celebrate with the new generation of each family a tradition set up a good 65 years ago by our wonderful Uncle Albert!

Chapter 19

LIFE AT HULL GRAMMAR SCHOOL (HGS)

I commented in an earlier chapter about the 11+ exams that we, as primary school pupils, had to take in the final year at Southcoates Primary School. The outcome of my good results in these exams was that I was awarded a place at Hull Grammar School, starting in their brand new building on Sept.1/1953, the very day that the school transferred to its new location at the end of Bishop Alcock Road, off Bricknell Avenue, to the west of Hull. The new facilities were an impressive sight for many of us, whose primary education was spread over 6 years in pre-WW1 buildings in very poor shape.

Above: View of the main entrance to Hull Grammar School in 1953
Below: The main classroom block seen from the sports fields

In my case, destiny seems to have favoured me in **not** being part of the "Hymer's experience", as I was extremely happy at Hull Grammar School, although certain classes did prove a "bind" to me. One in particular was P.E., where I was rather bad at climbing ropes and all other exercises where muscular strength might be required. I had always been a thin youngster, with little muscle, and as much as I made great efforts to please Mr. Wade (and later Mr. Garbutt) with the exercises they required from us, my body just didn't want to respond. This then would always prove to be a stumbling block to my overall scholastic performance.

At the end of the second year, the HGS had the custom of taking a number of pupils to the Rolston Summer Camp, just about 3 miles south of Hornsea, to integrate much more those of different backgrounds and from different parts of the city, who normally saw each other only during classes from 9am to 4pm. The ones who had enlisted to attend would spend about 4 or 5 days together in WW2-surplus huts, doing a series of special activities involving the countryside, much different from what went on in school.

I don't remember too much about the activities the teachers organised, but do recall that the experience didn't compare at all well with the Cub and Scout camps I had attended previously. Even the food was not nearly as good as what we would cook for ourselves on those other occasions. The only advantage was that we got to know several teachers (especially Mr. Leigh) in a much less formal atmosphere than at school.

Our history teacher at HGS (Mr. Ashworth) was a total bore, limiting his lessons to the reading of a huge book, covering ancient history up to the period around the birth of Christ. From what I can remember, never once in the two years he taught me did he spontaneously enlarge upon the subject we might be reading about! As a result, I took great exception to this subject, which was why I dropped it on starting my third year at HGS. Nevertheless, in later life, with the illustration that many TV documentaries provide, I have taken a great interest in History in general.

Our geography teacher, Mr. "Danny" Silverstone, was an excellent teacher in his subject. However, he had a habit that annoyed more than one in our classes – his obsession with writing all his work on the blackboards at a supersonic pace. As all his pupils had to copy these notes into our exercise books, this would cause great problems. On many occasions several of us would have to borrow someone else's book to complete their notes, since Danny's text would almost always have been wiped off the blackboards long before we'd finished copying. One of the principal negative results of these marathons was the total deterioration of my hand-writing over a period of two or three years!

It is only fair to pay tribute to my Maths teacher, Mr. "Digger" Leigh, despite the fact of his being disliked by many of my school colleagues. Mr. Leigh was a very sarcastic, but also very strict teacher. However, as maths has always come easy to me, I was one of his pupils who would receive a nickname from him, adopted later by Mr. Jackson in my Spanish lessons. In my case it was "Dy", as a result of my Welsh connections, a nickname that in other circumstances has been given to our son Dylan too.

My conclusion about Mr. Leigh is that one's inclination in favour or against him was directly proportional to one's facility or lack of it in Maths, as he would be rather nasty to those who didn't learn his lessons so easily. In my case, I took advantage of learning a whole series of mathematical "tricks" that Mr. Leigh would include in his classes. And I can guarantee that this ease of handling everyday mathematical problems really gave me a practical advantage in my working life.

Our English Language and Literature teacher, Mr. Page, probably the oldest of our teachers and the one with the longest service at HGS, was what one could call a perfect gentleman and a genuine authority on the English language. He left me with my great love of grammar and syntax, which in turn gave me a good logistical base when learning French and Spanish.

For most of the first 5 years in HGS to GCE level, we had Mr. Matthews as our French teacher. Although he was not Head of Modern Languages, he was a no-nonsense teacher with a very good technique, at least for our group of those with reasonably good language skills.

At the end of the second school year, all pupils had to make choices about which subjects to continue studying and which to drop. I ended up dropping History and taking the mix of "Physics with Chemistry" on the science side, though this subject never really inspired me at all.

Mr. Page with his Form 1B – May 1954
(I am second from left in the back row)

Having had the experience at my Junior School in the Carol Concert Choir, I volunteered for the HGS choir, directed by our music teacher, Mr. Graydon. He was very dedicated to his music, but had serious problems handling unruly members of our class, during music lessons. Our "performances" as a choir would be limited to special school events like Speech/Prize Days and the annual "Commemoration" Service, held at Holy Trinity at the end of each year.

On one occasion, I participated in the only theatrical event performed at the school over many years (see a later chapter). However, on a personal level, I continued with my participation in the combined Schools Choir every Christmas till 1957 at the Hull City Hall, a real pleasure at each Christmastide.

The Headmaster of HGS, Mr. J. Leslie Nightingale, during my years at the School

Our Headmaster, Mr. Nightingale ("the Boss"), a revered dour man, would take the classes of Divinity (as Religious Education was called in HGS). Why ever it was given that name was never explained to us. A note sent to anyone to be called to his office was almost always a bad omen – one had committed some sort of an offence against the school rules! Although there were between 720 and 750 pupils in his school, it was surprising that he could quietly keep himself up-to-date on so many individual pupils' achievements.

So far as I remember, I was only summoned to the Boss's office on two or three occasions, for pretty minor events. But the occasion I do remember with great satisfaction was when Mr. Nightingale wanted to reassure me of his support for Mr. Jackson's Spanish classes on my own, despite the fact that no-one else would be taking this subject to A Level. This trip to his office coincided with the beginning of my Sixth Form years. I had taken my O Level exams earlier in 1958, and had passed in English Language, French, Spanish, Maths, Geography and Physics with Chemistry, though I had failed in English Literature! This was a bit of a setback, since it was one of the 3 subjects I had chosen for entry into the "Arts" Sixth Form, as well as French and Spanish.

As this subject was the only one that fitted in with my Sixth Form timetable, I was admitted to the A Level Eng.Lit. Class, on the condition that I would re-sit and pass the O Level Eng.Lit. Exam in December that same year. This I did successfully and was thus allowed to continue with the A Level course in Eng. Lit, which I went on to pass in 1960.

On entering the Sixth Form, I had made it known to the teaching staff that I was aiming to go to university to study Romance Languages (at least that was my intention in 1958). However, at that moment in time, university admissions for this type of degree required knowledge of Latin, at least to O Level. Therefore, apart from cramming to take the Eng.Lit. O Level exam, I started to receive accelerated classes of Latin from Mr. Loughlin, who seemed to have been teaching Latin for ever at HGS. Eventually, I would pass the Latin exam completing what usually took 5 years to study in only four terms of classes. Thanks for that amazing feat, Mr. Loughlin!

Chapter 20

Tribute to a wonderful Teacher

In the first two years at HGS, I received French classes. Then it was in the third year that I had the unique chance of a lifetime to take Spanish at the age of 13, which left its mark for the rest of my life. I later came to know that at the time, no more than 200 school children in the whole of Britain were being taught Spanish, and of those, who knows how many really learnt it as intensely as I did.

I have described how I came to be part of the 1955 "experiment" with Spanish when I was 13 for being in the first 15 or 20 pupils of French in the previous year. So, it is fitting for me to pay a really heart-felt tribute to the person who, as Head of Modern Languages at HGS, would guide me to be more than usually proficient with Spanish and French at "A" Level, and lay the basis for my life abroad. That was Mr. Alfred H. Jackson ("Mad Alf", as he was known to the pupils), my close mentor in foreign languages. [Unfortunately, I have been unable to find a photo of him anywhere]

Mr. Jackson turned out to be an astonishing authority on the Spanish language and literature. As an Oxford graduate, he had taken Modern/Romance Languages at Oxford University, and did an MA in Madrid (Spain) (or possibly Salamanca – I could never determine the exact place) under Dámaso Alonso, who was later known for his long period as the Director of the Spanish Royal Language Academy.

At Oxford, Alf Jackson would meet up not only with Dámaso Alonso, but with the Spanish playwright, Federico Garcia Lorca, who was later assassinated by Franco's forces during the Spanish Civil War at the hands of a firing squad. Through this connection, in his student days, he would spend a lot of time in Spain with the "Generation of 99", a loosely formed group of authors and playwrights, who dominated Spain's literary scene in the mid to late 1930's, and whose "tertulias" (literary gatherings) he would attend in Madrid.

The Spanish "experiment" at HGS would only have 3 years to bring the 15 pupils who finally entered the class to GCE "O" level at the age of 16. So, the teaching was very intensive, under Mr. Jackson's severe style. He was, however, a great coach, and would use nicknames for many of the pupils whom he thought had any talent, in the same way as Mr. Leigh. Thus, I was always "Dy" to him, as a result of my Welsh origins.

Later, I would find out that Mr. Jackson seemed to have had a firm personal attachment to Wales, having retired to a lonely point in the Welsh mountains (a cottage called Maes Helen, near the village of Llanfaglan, Caenarfon in North Wales), as a kind of hermit's retreat. From there I would receive one single reply from him to a letter I wrote to him, asking me (for reasons I could never understand) NOT to contact him ever anymore! More than anything, he alleged that he never wanted to be reminded about Hull ever again, equally for reasons I didn't fathom!

I had got in touch with Mr. Jackson, through the good offices of "Danny" Silverstone, the HGS Geography teacher, during one of my return visits to HGS, when I would be on holiday in UK. On hindsight, obviously he should not have given me Mr. Jackson's address. However, my only intention was to let him know how grateful I was for all the time and effort he'd put into his part of my education, which had allowed me to do so much in life, all on the basis of the Spanish language, or "Castilian", as he would always insist.

In the Sixth Form, he would cram me with the more famous Spanish and Latin American Literature that he knew so well, starting with Fray Luis de León, El Mío Cid, El Quijote (Don Quixote), Federico Garcia Lorca, Unamuno, Ivan Darío and many more. Whenever a new Spanish word would crop up, this would be copied into a special notebook opposite its English translation and I would have the task of memorising the list each week for the next week's test. Although she had no idea of Spanish, my mother would help me at home giving me "tests" of each week's memory list. In this way, in Spanish alone, I would accumulate a vocabulary of more than 5,000 new words over the two years.

In French, which was also taught by Mr. Jackson in the Sixth Form, a similar situation would arise, though by the time A Levels came along, my preference towards Spanish as my favourite language was overwhelming. Funnily enough, I put up with the classes of A Level English Literature as a kind of necessary evil, since I needed a third subject pass to enter university, which eventually I never needed to do!

[As Prof. Stephen Hawking very recently commented: *"Behind every exceptional person, there is an exceptional teacher".*]

Final 6th Form photo at Hull Grammar School

Chapter 21

HGS & Marco Polo

In the winter of 1958, two of the teachers at Hull Grammar School (HGS), Mr. Fisher and Mr. Heron, decided that it was time to have our all-boys school more related to the nearby Newland High School, an all-girls grammar school at the time. The first joint event programmed for presentation in the Main Hall of HGS was a musical comedy written by these same two very talented teachers, called "Marco Polo", in which pupils of both schools would participate.

The show had three main scenes: the first representing Marco Polo in Italy before he set out for China; the second, his encounter with the Mongols during his voyage; and finally, Marco Polo in the emperor's palace in Peking (called Beijing these days). As a member of the school choir, I was recruited to form part of the chorus, first as an Italian nobleman, then a Mongol, and finally a Chinese courtesan, respectively in the three main acts. Great fun was had by all during the two performances we gave for the public, mainly made up of parents of the participants.

One of our school colleagues, Dave Tenney, was featured playing his guitar in the Mongol camp scene. A few years later, he would find a little fame as Dev Douglas a pop musician.

Unfortunately, I have not been able to track down any photos of this event, and a copy of the show's programme I had kept for many years, seems to have gone astray.

Chapter 22

CYCLING TO SCHOOL & A LONG JOURNEY TO BOURNEMOUTH

In my first years at HGS, I struck up a close friendship with two class colleagues, Tony Stubbs, who lived on the opposite (west) side of Hull, and Leslie (Les) Paling, who lived a little nearer me in the east on Gilshill Road, near Sutton, and with whom I shared the common interest of Scouting, as he was also a member of the troop at Sutton Church.

Once I was given my bicycle in 1954, Les and I would meet up on weekdays at around 8:30am near Stoneferry Bridge, to ride together the final 3 miles to school, come rain or snow! Being lazy at getting up in the morning, I would have to race along to manage to reach the school gates by the stroke of 9am. Thank goodness, the traffic was still scarce at that time!

Tony was a fellow member of the HGS School Choir and of the Orchestra, as he played the tuba and the saxophone. I would frequently exchange ideas with him on homework subjects and religious matters, since he was a devote member of the Salvation Army, and a very serious debater. We also had several interests in common, like classical music. By the time Tony was 15 or 16, he had been going out for some time with his girl-friend, Heather, the daughter of one of the Salvation Army leaders in Hull. However, earlier that year, the "Army" had moved her father to Bournemouth on the south coast.

Tony was "head over heels" with Heather and as he knew of my cycling interests (both to school and on the Scout cycling club outings), he invented a 270-mile cycling journey to Bournemouth and "recruited" me to accompany him during the summer school holidays to see his "beloved"! We were to camp out with a small tent in any friendly farmer's field that we would search out at the end of each day's long haul! If I remember right, it must have taken us at least 6 or maybe even 7 days to arrive at our destination, with many difficulties with camping at night. How and where we ate on the way, I just can't remember now. So, it must have been one of our minor problems.

We left Hull on the Humber Ferry, as this shortened the journey from the very start. Then we embarked on the long straight ride along the A15 towards Lincoln and Newark. My first startling impression came when we passed the area around Kirton in Lindsey, where I remember cycling up a hill to get a sudden view of a village, which I appeared to recognise in its every twist and turn (although I had never been on that road in my life before)! I don't now remember its name, but this is an experience I've never since been able to explain.

The following impression was of the beautiful Cathedral at Lincoln which we visited briefly as we passed through the city. Then on towards Newark and the A1, to find a field for the night, which was especially difficult on that first occasion. As we were in late July or early August, fortunately the weather was quite kind to us and we had only the occasional shower during our journey. Eventually, very worn out, we reached the south coast and our objective of Bournemouth, where we stayed a few days with Heather's family and spent some time on the beach recovering from the long hard ride.

We had planned for a total of two weeks away from home, but with the 6 or 7 days ride each way and a few days in Bournemouth, the 500+ mile "adventure" took a total of 16 or 17 days, an experience which I'm sure neither of us will ever forget! Needless to say, Tony married Heather a few years later.

With Les, in later years when I had acquired my first car, we would have a similar "adventure", this time in Spain, but this will be the subject of a chapter in Part 2.

Chapter 23

STUDENT EXCHANGE IN RURAL FRANCE

For the summer of 1958, HGS arranged for a group of those who were learning French in our year to travel to the region of Lille in France for a student exchange with youngsters from that area. As far as I now remember, we left England on a ferry from Dover to Boulogne, where we caught a train destined for Lille. There I was met by Jean-Claude Thomas and his father, who drove me to their home in the village of Grand Verly, near Vadencourt, in the northern French Department of Aisne, a good hour and a half from Lille. Jean-Claude's jolly mother was Marie (I believe), and he had two younger sisters, Jocelyn and Ghislaine, about 13 and 10 or 11 at the time.

The Thomas's family house in Grand Verly (Aisne)

I was one of the few boys to be sent to a rural area, a village of probably no more than 500 people, or maybe less. Even at that time, 13 years after the end of the war, France had still not recovered from the effects of the years of the German occupation. Conditions in rural areas were still very rudimentary with running water only on the ground floor of the houses.

The whole country was subject to petrol rationing; so, although M. Thomas, as the local mayor's secretary, was the only person in the village with a car, he was able to take me out to neighbouring tourist sites on just two occasions, since he would only receive something like 20 litres (4.2 UK gallons) of petrol **per month** for all his journeys. So, unfortunately, Paris was too far for his petrol ration.

Early every morning, I would be taken for a walk with M. Thomas and his son Jean-Claude the mile or so to the centre of the village to collect the family's daily ration of no less than 12 or 15 baguettes, the bread that the family would consume each and every day. My recollections of the rest of the food are very hazy.

The Thomas Family in 1958

What I do remember very well were the rowdy sessions of card games I would sit in on many afternoons and evenings, when M. Thomas and Jean-Claude would gather round a table with friends from the village, shouting a lot and banging the table with their fists to make a point. As, of course, my comprehension of spoken French was still quite rudimentary, then most of the time I understood only a fraction of what was going on!

Once my 3 weeks in France were over, Jean-Claude travelled with me to spend his own 3 weeks in England at our house in Hull. I know we did quite a lot of tourism (probably to York, Beverley, Bridlington and Scarborough) whilst he was there, but the details completely escape me! However, Jean-Claude was a very reserved person and never really revealed whether he enjoyed his stay in England or not. He seemed to get on well with my parents and appeared to enjoy the food we gave him, though I imagine he missed his baguettes an awful lot!

After our exchange, I would maintain occasional correspondence with Jean-Claude for maybe 6 or 8 years, but after he started work, he eventually moved to a different area of France and I lost contact with him for good. His parents and later his sisters would receive the Christmas cards I would continue to send to the family in Grand Verly over the years, and later they would take up our correspondence on the internet.

In 2012, Ghislaine asked me to organise for her daughter, Hélène, a short overseas student's English course in the city of York, which I duly did. And I now understand that this has helped her a lot in her university studies and the job she has subsequently taken.

Chapter 24
A Scouting & Church Background

Here it's probably important to note that my father was in charge of the St. Aidan's Scout Group for many years. He was originally a member of the St. Columba's Scout Group in his youth, but I assume that, when St. Aidan's Church was being built, he helped organise the new Scout group there. One of my aunts (Vera, my Dad's sister) was the Akela (adult leader) of the Cub pack, with lots of help from her husband Jim.

As a result of all this family involvement, being the first grandchild on either side of our two families, by the time I was 5 or 6, they had me attending the Cub Pack meetings on Tuesday evenings. Although officially Cubs were not received until the age of 8, I was described as their "mascot" which allowed me to be present, and even at the age of 6 or 7, I was taken to their annual camp at farm in Skeffling, a few miles to the east of Hull on the road to Spurn Point, accompanied by my Mother.

The Cub Pack with Harry Armstrong, Uncle Jim Penny & my Aunt Vera, with me, then Ralph Oldfield at the back next to Harry

Not long after the WW2, the Scouts had raised funds to buy their own "hut" (a war surplus building), which my father personally rebuilt on the side of St. Aidan's Church with the help of several of other Scouts' parents and some of the older Scouts themselves. As a teenager, the family tie gave me access to the Scout Hall during school holidays, together with many of my friends (though I have certain doubts that Ralph was part of the group of friends who took advantage of this). There we would keep ourselves warm in those hard winters, stoking up the wood/coke stoves, which would glow red hot when in full fury! We would play table tennis, cards, billiards and all sorts of things, which kept us occupied, rather than being at a loose end on the street.

Scouting friends: Derek Close, me, David Fowler, Trevor Coleman and David Brookes

After we progressed to the Scout Troop on reaching the age of eleven, Ralph and I (so far as I recall) also attended the annual weeklong camp in 1954, which would have been in WW2 tents probably in Derbyshire. My memory now doesn't distinguish too well which year we went to the different areas where the Troop chose to camp, sometimes in Derbyshire, other times in the North York

Moors or Wolds, and once in the Lake District. At that time, it was still possible to pack all our gear and even ourselves (15 or 20 Scouts plus the Scout Master Howard Richardson, Bruce Leng and a couple of other leaders) into the back of a lorry (see photo) and trundle over 80 or 100 miles to our destination without any problem.

View of the Cub pack with Jim Penny in the foreground about to leave for their 1950 Annual Camp

I don't recall too well how these summer camps were financed, though I believe we (or probably more correctly, our parents) all had to pay in a fixed sum some time before the week we would depart. The Scout Parents' Committee would always play an important role in all these events, raising funds to finance different activities. I remember that the Higgins and the Woods were two of the many families who worked tirelessly to raise the necessary funds for these activities, as also my two Aunts Muriel and Dinky.

The Scout Hall at St. Aidan's was an almost entirely wooden building of about 8 metres wide by 25 metres long, plus a small stage at the eastern end. It had been acquired through the fund raising efforts of the Parents' Committee in the late 1940s as (I believe) war surplus. It was dismantled from its original site and shipped to Southcoates Avenue, where it was re-assembled under my father's guidance. Over the years, it was subject to the harsh Hull weather, springing lots of leaks, naturally suffering considerable deterioration and a serious fire at one moment. So, in the mid-50s, funds were again raised to have a steel structure inserted to reinforce the frame and allow the roof to be renewed.

As a result of my activities with the Scouts, a group of friends arose almost spontaneously from among the members of the Troop, including Howard Croft, David Fowler, David Brookes, Malcolm Gardner and myself. We would form a close-knit unit during our teenage years, meeting up at first at the Scout Hall and later at each others' houses with our respective girl-friends.

As time went by, we would go out together to our favourite pubs, not only in Hull but once we had our own transport, to neighbouring villages, like Melton, Skirlaugh, Wawne, Beverley and Bishop Burton etc. Both at St. Aidan's Sunday School, where we all attended, as also at the Girl Guides, we met several girls, including Carol Nasby and her sister Susan, who would become permanent members of our "group of friends", until they went off to university after the age of 18.

Chapter 25

St. Aidan's, Our local Church

One of the people whom I remember very well from those days was the curate who was sent to be in charge of St. Aidan's church around 1951, before it was consecrated as an independent parish. He was Rev. Roger Robinson, a fairly young person at the time, who was highly esteemed by all worshippers. He became the Vicar of the new parish in 1954, and stayed with us well into the 60's, before being sent on to a parish near Leeds, I believe.

The reason why I mention him is that, apart from being our spiritual guide, he was a very good friend of our family. I am proud to have been able to correspond with him (mainly through the exchange of Christmas cards) ever since I left Hull. On arriving in England for Christmas of 2011, I was delighted to find a new letter of his waiting for me at Emlyn's house. His sight deteriorated over time, but he still occasionally gave sermons in a Leeds parish near his retirement home. Whilst I was starting to write this book, I sadly received news of his death in February 2016 at the age of 92.

St Aidan's Church was originally built in the 1930's with funds raised through dances, whist drives, bingos etc. by many locals, including both my father's and my mother's families. The church was small to start with, but was extended in the late 1950's, being originally a dependency of the parish of St. Columba's, where my parents had to be married, as St. Aidan's was not consecrated for marriages in 1937.

According to a note I recently found on the web,
"Services were first held at 77 College Grove in 1924 and a temporary church opened in 1925. The first part of the permanent church was dedicated in 1935. It was consecrated in 1955 and was given a new district taken from parishes of Drypool, Marfleet and St Michael in 1954."

St. Aidan's became the focal point of our family life, since, in their spare time, my parents would devote many hours to different organisations which revolved around the church or derived from it. My father was first a Scout, then a Rover (when over 16) at St. Columba's, before finally becoming Scoutmaster in the Scout Group which was formed as part of St. Aidan's youth activities.

My mother was first a teacher at the church's Sunday School, and in her late 20's took over the running of the part of the Sunday School which taught children about the Church and the Bible from about 3 or 4 to 10 years of age. Eventually, she would devote more than 25 years of her life to this voluntary work until her death in 1967. In the same way, she would spend a lot of time supporting my father's Scouting work, with the organisation of a whole myriad of fund-raising events through the Parents' Committee of the Scout Group.

Around the time when I would be 10 or 11, there were many Scout Groups in different parts of Hull. As a result, it was decided to divide up the area which the city-wide Scout Commissioner covered to form three more localised areas: North, West and South East Hull, and my father was invited to assume the position of South East Hull Scout Commissioner. He jumped at this opportunity, despite having his hands full already with the running of the St.

Aidan's Scout Group, which he didn't relinquish till many years later. Adding to this, around that time, he volunteered as an usher at the Sunday Church services, and eventually became Churchwarden on the laymen's Parish Council. This group of laymen would meet once a month to organise the church finances and other topics related to its daily running.

The complete St. Aidan's Scout Group with Parent Supporters (around 1952)

With all these responsibilities (all voluntary and non-paid), on weekdays my father would arrive home from work around 5:30pm, have his evening meal, scan a newspaper, and then head off almost immediately (before 7pm.) for one of his numerous meetings or visits to other Scout Groups. Thus, he was rarely at home for very long. On the other hand, weekends would see him in the garden, weeding, planting and otherwise tending to the produce and flowers he maintained there, including the strawberries and tomatoes, which I would help him with for watering and weeding.

Chapter 26

A TV SET FOR THE CORONATION (JUNE 2ND, 1953)

The year 1952 saw the death of King George VI in February, and the accession to the throne of Queen Elizabeth II, previously Princess Elizabeth. Britain had made its initial efforts to rebuild the country after the War finished 7 years earlier, but there was still a great deal to be done. Housing, especially, was in a bad shape, and food was still being rationed.

Although there was much debate about whether the Queen's Coronation in 1953 should be held so lavishly at a time when the country was still facing many hardships, and especially after the death of the Queen's own grandmother, Queen Mary. Even after considering all these factors, the government decided to go ahead, allowing the ceremony to be televised for the first time in history. On 2 November 1936, the BBC had begun transmitting the world's first public regular high-definition service from the Victorian Alexandra Palace in north London. On 1 September 1939, two days before Britain declared war on Germany, the station was taken off air with little warning, and only returned to regular service in 1945 initially in the south-east of England. This was extended to Birmingham by 1949 and the whole country was being covered by the mid-1950's. As a result of the Coronation, the amount of homes with a new TV set was given an instant boom.

Only two months before the Coronation, my grandfather Fred had died on March 23rd, just one day before the death of Queen Mary. However, our family was no stranger to the television trend. As a result, Auntie Dinky and Uncle Albert decided to buy a TV set not long before the great event, so that the whole family could watch it together on June 2nd, 1953.

Chapter 27

FROM CARPENTER TO BUILDER'S MANAGER

Not content with so much voluntary work, my father had always had his sights set on working as an architect or builder as a career. However, in the far off days around 1926 or 27 (not long before the Great Depression of 1929), he would have left school at the age of 14 or 15 (as was perfectly normal in those days), but opportunities for adolescents were far from abundant. So, his choice of carpentry meant becoming an apprentice to a "time-served" expert in that area, who would make the family a monthly charge for teaching Harold his trade, probably for a total of three years. During this period of practical training, he also attended evening classes to acquire theoretical knowledge of carpentry and also several other subjects related to the building trade which would be the basis for his future career.

Once Harold finished his apprenticeship in (maybe) 1930, he would eventually go to work for Priestman's, a local company based in the East of Hull, becoming a foreman joiner (carpenter) a few years later. In this position, (although I'm not sure whether at Priestman's or Hollis's, where he also worked - *see leaflet overleaf*) my father would get married in 1937 and have his son (me) in 1942. However, his ambitions for further promotion in his career most certainly were stopped in their tracks by the outbreak of WW2 in 1939.

What I do know is that in approximately 1953 or 54, having worked in at least two other firms, my father took the post of Builder's Manager in R. Finch Sons & Co. Ltd. This was a fairly small family company whose offices were on Hedon Road, just before the Saltend roundabout, opposite what is now the huge Saltend oil refinery. In its beginnings Finch's would be dedicated to supplying carpentry services to different types of building developments. Then, in the early 1950's, the company would start building small batches of houses.

Later, in 1954 or 55 (I estimate) they won the contract to build Hull's new Central Police Station at one side of Queen's Gardens, which opened in the Spring of 1957. This was definitely the high point of my father's career, where he would oversee the building of this important city centre development, which formed part of the general renovation of Hull's City Centre. There had been so much severe bomb damage that the area was only slowly being redeveloped over the first 15 years after the end of the War.

One amazing aspect of the Police Station development was that during the early stage of laying the foundations, my father would come home to tell us of the "total loss" of several of the pylons, which were needed to give the building sufficient extra support, since it had been situated on the side of the former Queen's Dock. The pylons would simply disappear in the process of being hammered into the area of the building's foundations, and would need additional pylons placed on top of each one until the required support was guaranteed.

Two different views of the Central Police Station, built by
R. Finch Sons & Co. Ltd.

Around that time, my father was invited to occupy for a year the position as Head of the local chapter of the Hull Guild of Building, a real honour for one whose career had started as an apprentice carpenter. This was most certainly the high point of his whole career.

Eventually, sometime after my father retired in 1977, the R. Finch Sons & Co. would be acquired by Scruton's, another local firm of long standing in Hull's building trade, and was merged into this bigger organisation.

Chapter 28

LEAVING SCHOOL WITH DOUBTS ABOUT THE FUTURE

I sat the GCE A Level exams in May and June 1960 in the midst of a growing dilemma about my future. I had investigated the career opportunities for a Romance Languages graduate, and found that virtually the only real job prospect at the time was to become a teacher. But I had absolutely no vocation for teaching! Similarly, my mother's aspirations for having a doctor in the family were a long way away from my own inklings. I had really never had much of an interest in sciences, and had only taken classes in "Physics with Chemistry", a kind of summarised introduction to these areas, as a type of filler to comply with the number of subjects I was required to take at HGS. Being in the B stream, we never had the opportunity to take Biology, as I believe those in the A stream did. So, the chance of steering myself toward a career in medicine was very remote and far from representing a vocation for me.

In the months just after the A level exams, I decided to explore other possibilities, different from a university career. So, I applied to the Foreign Office to enter the Diplomatic Service, where I thought my languages could be a great advantage to a possible career. However, this entailed taking the Civil Service exams, which I duly did in June of 1960. I was extremely pleased when I got the results, since I had come out in the 29th place out of more than 900 school leavers, who had taken these exams. This exempted me from the first of two levels of interviews.

Not long after receiving the results, I was summoned to appear in Whitehall, at the Foreign Office, where I would be interviewed by a panel of top Civil Servants. At the age of 18, I had had no experience of this type of grilling, and no-one in the family could have given me much warning of what might happen. Having gone down to London early in the morning on the train, I crossed the city from King's Cross to the Westminster tube station, and walked the few yards to the venue of the interview. There I was greeted by the staff organising the interviews, and asked to sit in the waiting room, before my turn came up. No-one indicated to me exactly what I could expect.

When the time came to walk into the interview room, I was dismayed to find myself sitting on a lone chair about 12 to 15 yards away from a long table, confronted with no less than 15 people behind it. I was grilled with a whole series of questions, though, frankly, I now don't remember any of the details of the conversation! However, I do remember facial expressions from the interviewers when a voice with a Hull accent started to give the replies. It became obvious in a very short while that my provincial accent was distinctly NOT what the very elitist Foreign Office staff wanted at that moment in time (1960).

Shortly afterwards, I received the more or less expected letter, saying that I did not qualify for the Foreign Office, but that they could offer me a whole series of positions in either the Estate Duty Office (ironically where my great Uncle George had been the boss only a few years before), the Inland Revenue or other parts of central government. I researched possibilities in several of these openings, but didn't find any to my liking. This left me in a serious dilemma, but, in the end, I consider they did me a real favour.

I was beginning to get a bit nervous about what I would do in September 1960, after school was behind me. I had ruled out Romance Languages at university, and the Diplomatic Corps had ruled me out. So, what else could I look for? One of the contacts I had developed in my teenage years was a slightly older acquaintance (Cyril Young) at the Scouts who worked in the Spectrometry Laboratory at Reckitt's and also played in the company table tennis team.

As this was my favourite sport, I had volunteered to play for one of the Reckitt's team as a hobby for some three years before leaving school. Therefore, I had been in touch with a few people at Reckitt's and learned that they and many other big companies had international divisions, which probably employed people with foreign languages. So, I decided to try my luck with applications to about a dozen multinationals, including Unilever (at that time Lever Brothers), BP, Glaxo and Reckitt's.

To be very honest, apart from one formal acknowledgement, the only positive reply I ever received was from Reckitt's, whose world HQ was in Hull, not all that far from where our family lived. Although one of my father's cousins (Eric Beeston) was the Chief Cashier of the company, we rarely had contact with him, and I had no idea he worked there. So, when the interview day came in late July 1960, I went along with only the knowledge of the company I had gained from the fellow table tennis colleagues, in whose team I had been playing for two or three years, and from my father, who also knew a few people who worked there.

I now recall very little of the details of the interview, except that it went very well, and concentrated a lot on my knowledge of Spanish. Reckitt's International Department (Reckitt & Colman Overseas Ltd.) had several regional sections, including one that covered Latin America and Spain. This was headed up by a Regional Director (at that time Kenneth Clark) who formed part of the Overseas Board, and would travel a lot to keep tabs on the different local factories in the region. On the second floor of the Hull office, each of these regional directors would have a Personal Assistant and a Secretary. At that moment, there was a vacancy for a new P/A to the Director for Latin America.

A view of the Reckitt & Colman Offices showing the one I would occupy on the second floor

One of the P/A's job requirements was a good broad knowledge of Spanish, which could be turned into fluency in the language. I do remember that at one part of the interview I had to translate a letter that had arrived from one of Reckitt's distributors in Ecuador, Bolivia, Paraguay or the Canary Islands (though I don't remember which!). I must have done this pretty well, since everything finished off very warmly, and I was told I would receive a letter from them regarding the job in the next few days. I did however express my need to complete my further education with an appropriate qualification, which would complement my career.

The letter duly arrived the following week, offering me the post of P/A to the Director for Latin America, with effect from 5th September 1960. I would be allowed to work from 9am to 4pm. (not 5pm, as was usual) in order to have enough time to devote myself to my Diploma in Business Studies. This I would take as an evening course at the Hull College of Commerce & Technology (as it was called then), whose classes finished at 8 or 9pm each evening.

My school days were over!

Chapter 29
CHILDHOOD STICKING POINT

Whether as a result of the stress of the War, the trauma of my near drowning in Bridlington or who knows what, around the age of 6 or 7, I developed a stutter that seemed to get worse as I went through the primary school. This would make me rather withdrawn and reluctant to make many friends at that time.

However, one of the distractions that appealed to me was the pleasure of singing. So, in 1952, when I was approached by Mr. Metcalfe, the Music teacher at Southcoates Primary School to take part in the first Annual Joint Schools Carol Concert at the City Hall, I jumped at the chance. There would be a lot of rehearsals for at least two months at our own school before the concert dates (usually for two nights during the second or third week of December), and then one or two more at the City Hall itself with all 350 children gathered together to finalise the presentation.

To help overcome my stutter, my mother arranged appointments with several speech therapists, who would put me through different verbal exercises. Although these consultations did help my problem to a certain extent, they didn't seem to make the significant difference that the passage of time would prove to do.

Recently this comment came to my attention:

<< *Some people admit that having learned a new language has allowed them to feel more self-confident, more open, more tolerant and more creative. The fact of being able to find an alternative way of saying the things, of expressing a concept when the word that we want to say is on the tip of the tongue, can produce fantastic and very original creations!* >>

As I entered the secondary school (Hull Grammar School) I also would discover foreign languages. This exercise in new types of pronunciation and my success, first in French, and then in Spanish, seemed to do marvels for my stutter, as it gradually disappeared as a major difficulty in life. This allowed me to make many more friends and acquaintances, and to socialise much more in general. With time I started to regain much more self assurance to face first the Civil Service exams and the London interview and then finally the interview at Reckitt & Colman (Overseas), which would change the whole course of my adult life.

Chapter 30

REFLEXIONS ON A GRAMMAR SCHOOL EDUCATION

The English secondary school system in the 1950's and 60's was based on se-lection of pupils at the age of 11, according to their aptitude for the basic skills of reading, writing, maths and a certain amount of general knowledge, regard-less of their social background. This meant that many working class children would have the chance of a place in what some politicians have come to call "elite schools". Whether or not those exams devised for children of that age were or could be effective in selecting the appropriate youngsters for academic tuition is a matter for the experts, who seem to have very differing opinions on the subject. As Derek Gillard has said in his recent brief history of Education in England:

<< *Wilson (the Prime Minister in 1965) was anxious to increase opportunity with-in society. In the education system this meant change and expansion: for the first time ever, a British government spent more on education than on defence. There was a significant increase in the number of university places, with more women under-taking higher education courses.*

But Wilson's record on secondary education was disappointing: while the pro-portion of children attending comprehensive schools rose to thirty per cent during this period, his government, like Attlee's in the post-war years, failed to establish a fully comprehensive system and selection survived. >>

The Labour Party had maintained for many years that the selective education system reinforced class division and upper and middle-class privilege. Howev-er, the high proportion of non-middle class pupils who have benefitted from this emphasis on more academic education is very significant. Therefore, one must ask: Why level **DOWN** the teaching with the comprehensive system, if the teaching staff has in any case to make special arrangements for different levels of learning abilities?

Where would Britain be in this 21st Century without the thousands of non-middle class pupils who went through the Grammar Schools and have occupied prominent places both in politics, industry, the Civil Service and the professions? My aim (if I were a politician) would be to level **UP** all the present comprehensive schools towards the standards of Grammar Schools and the Academies constituted in the last 6 or 8 years.

The government argues that academies drive up standards by putting more power in the hands of head teachers over pay, length of the school day and term times. They have more freedom to innovate and can opt out of the national curriculum. However, the latest moves to reintroduce more Grammar Schools must be extremely clear on their role within the present system to be successful.

Chapter 31

MY GROUP OF FRIENDS AND OUR EVENTUAL BREAK-UP

About the time when I was 15, a group of eight friends had arisen from mutual friendships at the St. Aidan's Scouts and the Church Sunday School. It was composed of the four boys mentioned earlier (David Fowler, David Brookes, Howard Croft and I, the eldest of the four), plus Carol Nasby, her sister Susan and two other girls, who varied from time to time. Later, we would be sometimes joined by Malcolm Gardner and a girl-friend he would have now and again.

We would often meet at one of our homes, usually on a Saturday evening to listen to music, chat and play special games. By the time I had left school, we were sometimes also going to one of the local pubs for a drink. As time went by, when I bought my first car and then David Fowler got one too, we would have regular outings to pubs, not only in Hull, but also in neighbouring villages. One of our favourite spots was the "Green Dragon" at Welton.

I was very fond of Carol at the time and considered her to be my "girl-friend" for several years. I was always very welcome at her home by her widowed mother and struck up what seemed to be a lasting friendship with the family. Having started work with Reckitt's in 1960, when they sent me for my 6 months' scholarship in Spain in 1962, I would exchange letters with Carol every two or three weeks (despite the disastrous postal service) and she would send replies to me wherever I happened to be on my travels.

However, when I arrived back in Hull after my 6 months' stay in Spain ready to celebrate Christmas with the family and Carol, I was confronted with the devastating fact that, in my absence, she had formed a close friendship with one of my "best friends", Howard Croft, with whom she would get married several years later. I was deeply affected and took a long time to overcome this unexpected turn of events. Our group of friends continued to gather together for outings to pubs etc., and although I would usually join them for those nights out, this only made matters worse for me, with a markedly uncomfortable feeling.

After I left for Colombia in 1966, most of us kept in touch by post at first with fairly regular correspondence. In 1970, I even travelled to California, spending several days with David Brookes, who was working there with an American computer company at the time (Honeywell, I believe). However, as time passed, each of us has gone his/her own way, and now, we have little if any contact. And the final irony was that Carol and Howard had two children (I believe), but got divorced after something like 30 years of marriage.

Looking back on that period, I conclude that the early months of 1963 saw the beginning of a total change in my life, which would evolve in 1966 with my posting to Cali, Colombia. However, the events leading up to, and following this huge milestone in my life, will be the subject of Part 2 of this narrative.

In PART 2, I will recount my early working years in England, my wonderful 6 months in Spain, my transfer to Colombia, my marriage and family, our numerous ventures and my eventual retirement to Dapa.

Appendix

A BRIEF HISTORY OF KINGSTON UPON HULL & WORLD WAR II BOMB DAMAGE SCENES

BRIEF HISTORY

Kingston upon Hull, the city I was born in, was founded by King Edward 1 in 1293, when the two districts, then known as Wyke and Myton, were purchased by the King. The city was originally called Kingstown upon Hull.

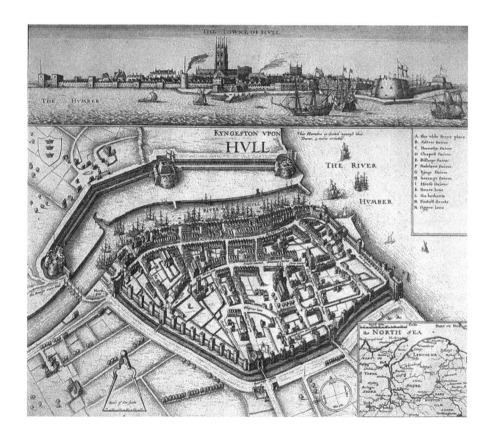

Hull, or to give it its full, correct name of Kingston upon Hull, is a medium sized city situated on the north bank of the River Humber. It is divided into two by the River Hull, hence the origin of its name. The area on the west side of the river is known as West Hull and on the eastern side of the river as East Hull. The area now known as North Hull was mainly developed in the early and middle 20th Century. The old City of Hull was encircled by the town walls, though nothing today remains of these but a very small section. The town grew and grew outside of the walls, spreading in all directions except the south, which was of course not possible because of the River Humber.

Hull has an annual Fair, now held in the month of October. The first charter to grant Hull a Fair was in 1278 but it was Edward I that granted a six week fair in May and June in 1293. In those days it was an economic event where trade was done and products bought and sold. By Charles II's time it had moved to 20th September. It was in 1751 when the change of calendar in use forcibly moved the date to October. Eleven days were lost from the year and there were minor riots in Hull as they thought that their Fair might be cut short. The people were placated and the Fair was made into a weeklong event that would start on the Friday that included the 11th October and ended on the following Saturday.

Over the years the Fair slowly began to include more entertainment and less trade. By the 18th and 19th Century the shows included jugglers and puppet shows and also wild animal shows where the people of Hull were able to observe beasts from far afield.

The Fair has moved around the city over the years. In the 1800's it was held in the Wellington, Nelson and Queen Street area near the pier and in the Market Place. It was also held outside the town on the Brown Cow fields before moving to Corporation Fields on Park Street in 1865.

The Fair continued to grow but it was never popular with the local residents and eventually it moved again to its present site at Walton Street in 1888. It was originally an 8 acre site but in 1906 it doubled in size making it the largest in Britain. By the late 1800's mechanisation brought more and more rides to the Fair and this continues to be up dated and gets faster, higher and more spectacular to this day. In 1908 there were 27 special railway excursions from far and wide bringing 12,000 people to the festivities. Electricity brought another element to the show and it was called the Light City. In 1919 there were twenty rides and now there are many many more.

In the very early part of the 1900s, there was widespread demolition of much of the old city (which consisted of slum housing) to create new wide streets, now known as King Edward Street and Jameson Street. Queen Victoria Square was built on the site once covered by Waterworks Street, St John's Street, Engine Street and Junction Street. Further pre-Victorian slum houses were demolished in the early 1930s, from an area from the corner of Beverley Road/Spring Bank to Anlaby Road to form what is now Ferensway (named after the local city benefactor, T. R. Ferens). Many of the people who lived in the slums were moved into the new housing estate to the north of the city, which became known as North Hull Estate.

Hull was severely bombed during the Second World War, with severe loss of life and much of the city centre was turned to ruins. Hull was proportionally the most severely bombed British city during the Second World War. There were 86 German air raids, the first on 19 June 1940 and the last on 17 March 1945. 86,715 buildings were damaged and 95 per cent of houses were damaged or destroyed. Of a population of around 320,000 at the beginning of the war, approximately 152,000 were made homeless as a result of bomb destruction or damage. Almost 1,200 people were killed and 3,000 injured. Much of the city centre was completely destroyed and heavy damage was inflicted on residential areas, industry, the railways and the docks. After the war the city centre was rebuilt to its present modern style.

As early as 1316 a ferry service was operating between Hull and Barton (Lincolnshire), while the more modern ferries across the River Humber to New Holland began in 1826 and carried on until 1981. A new ferry service between Hull and Rotterdam (Europoort), operated by North Sea Ferries, began in 1965.

In the fourteenth century, Hull handled much of England's wool trade and by the eighteenth century the importation of timber. Whaling was also important to Hull. Fishing had always been very important to Hull, with several hundred trawlers operating out of the port in any one year. Several docks were purposely built for the fishing industry. Hull was once the third largest port in England and at one time boasted no fewer than eleven docks. The earliest was Old Dock (later renamed Queen's Dock), opened in August 1778. Sadly now only four docks remain in use; the others have been converted to gardens, a marina, shopping centre, or new housing.

Beverley Gate (the remains of which can still be seen to this day at one end of Whitefriargate) was the site of the Lock Gates that linked the Queens Dock (now Queen's Gardens) with the Prince's Dock. When it was uncovered, the City Council moved the motion in the Council Chamber to keep the remains on show for people could see the site where King Charles I was denied entry to the then Town.

More importantly, he was denied access to the second largest Arsenal in the country located in the Citadel on the Eastern Banks of the River Hull after the one in the Tower of London. He needed access to get his hands on the huge stock of armaments stored there. The reason this huge Arsenal was located here in what was then the relatively small town of Kingston upon Hull, was its location, approximately halfway between the Tower of London with the biggest Arsenal, and what was at the time the enemy of the Scottish Clans. The munitions could be rushed up to Scotland to put down the latest uprising by the Clans in half the time it would take to get them from the Tower of London.

Because Hull expanded outside the town walls, road transport was required to transport people into the town. The earliest to operate were horse-drawn buses, which were followed in 1875 by horse-drawn trams operated by the Hull Street Tramways Co. This in turn gave way to the electric tramway which first operated on 5 July 1899 on two routes from St John Street, one down Anlaby Road.

Bomb Damage Scenes

Hull's first air-raid warning was at 02:45 on Monday 4th September 1940. As an 'air-raid yellow' all operational crews were called to their posts. The public siren sounded at 03:20 and the all-clear sounded at 04:08. No raid occurred.

- Number of raids (in which incendiaries and high explosives were dropped): 82
- Total number of people killed, as far as is known: 1,200
- Injured and received treatment: 3000
- Total damage incidents: 146,568
- Houses damaged: 86,715 (leaving only 5,945 undamaged)
- People rendered temporarily homeless and provided for: 152,000
- Number of alerts: 815
- Hours under alerts (more than): 1,000
- 250 domestic and 120 communal shelters were destroyed, from which more than 800 people were rescued alive.

The last raid on Hull happened on March 17 1945. At this late stage in the war, with Nazi Germany close to defeat, most people assumed the raids were over. So when the air raid sirens did sound at 9.35pm, there was widespread confusion and panic. Residents ran for cover as bombs began to drop over East Hull.

Nornabell Street, Barnsley Street, Victor Street, Balfour Street, Sherburn Street, Morrill Street and Holderness Road taking the brunt of the raid. Holderness Road, outside the Savoy Cinema, was described by eyewitnesses as "a river of blood". The dead were laid out at the top of Severn Street and hospitals were put on alert across Hull. Two days later the Mail reported that 12 had been killed and a further 22 injured. A memorial now stands outside the Boyes' store.

Lightning Source UK Ltd.
Milton Keynes UK
UKHW02f1229020318
318753UK00002B/7/P